The Charlton Standard Catalogue Canadian Tire Cash Bonus Coupons

2ND EDITION

By
Ross W. Irwin

W. K. Cross
Publisher

TORONTO, ONTARIO ✦ BIRMINGHAM, MICHIGAN

EDITORIAL

Editor   W. K. Cross
Assistant Editor   Jean Dale
Editorial Assistant   Janet Cross
Layout   Frank van Lieshout

ACKNOWLEDGEMENTS

The publisher would like to thank Don Robb and Walter Allan for contributing to this publication by reviewing the manuscript and data.

INSTITUTIONS

The Canadian Tire Coupon Collectors Club was formed in September 1991. Write the Club at P. O. Box 1000, Arkell, Ontario, N0B 1C0, for information.

COPYRIGHT AND TRADEMARK NOTICE

Copyright © Canadian Tire Corporation

The Triangle, the Scotsman, the Tire and Dollar logos and the design of the coupons all form part of the trademarks and copyrights of the Canadian Tire Corporation and must not be copied or reproduced without the written permission of the Corporation.

Copyright © 1994 Charlton International Inc. All Rights Reserved

The terms Charlton, Charlton's, The Charlton Press, the Charlton Catalogue Numbering System, Charlton Numbers and abbreviations thereof, are trademarks of Charlton International Inc. and shall not be used without written consent from Charlton International Inc.

While every care has been taken to ensure accuracy in the compilation of the data in this catalogue, the publisher cannot accept responsibility for typographical errors.

No part of this publication, including the CHARLTON CATALOGUE NUMBERING SYSTEM used herein, may be reproduced, stored in a retrieval system, or transmitted in any form or by any means, electronic, mechanical, photocopying, recording, or otherwise, without the prior written permission of the copyright owner.

No copyright material may be used without written permission in each instance from Charlton International Inc. Permission will be liberally given for the use of the CHARLTON CATALOGUE NUMBERING SYSTEM and initials for all coupons and varieties by anyone wishing to do so, including their use in advertisement of coupons for sale provided Charlton receives proper acknowledgement in each instance.

Permission is hereby given for brief excerpts to be used for the purpose of reviewing this publication in newspapers, magazines, periodicals and bulletins, other than in the advertising of items for sale, providing the source of the material so used is acknowledged in each instance.

```
Canadian Cataloguing in Publication Data
Main entry under title:
The Charlton standard catalogue of Canadian
Tire cash bonus coupons
1st ed. (1991) -
Biennial.
ISSN 1183-7098
ISBN 0-88968-164-3 (2nd ed.)
1. Canadian Tire Corporation. II. Title:
Canadian Tire cash bonus coupons.
CJ4914.C442       769.5'5     C92-030156-8
```

Printed in Canada
in the Province of Quebec

Editorial Office
2010 Yonge Street
Toronto, Canada M4S 1Z9
Telephone (416) 488-4653 Fax: (416) 488-4656

CONTENTS

Introduction v
Company History v
Company Logo vi
Cash Bonus Coupons vi
Printing Sequence viii
Grading ix
Specimen Coupons x
Replacement Coupons x
Special Number Coupons x
Number System x

GAS BAR COUPONS

CT1	First Issue — 1958, Rural Scene With CT Store	2
CT2	Second Issue — 1961, Map of Canada With Gas Bar 7 CTC Store ...	5
	CT2-1 Two Serial Numbers in Red	6
	CT2-2 One Serial Number in Red or Black	7
	CT2-3 No Serial Number on Face or Back	9
CT3	Third Issue — 1961, Modified Map of Canada	10
	CT3-1 Centre Serial Number in Red Below, Sasaki/Billes	12
	CT3-2 Centre Serial Number in Red Above, Sasaki/Billes	15
	CT3-3 Centre Serial Number in Red Above, Heuman/Groussman ..	17
CTM1	"Hercules" Gas War Coupon	19
CTM2	XV Cents Gas War Coupon	21
CTM3	Courtesy Corners Coupns	23
CTM4	Toronto Oil or Greasing Coupon	25

STORE COUPONS

CT21	First Issue — 1961, Seal Design	28
CT22	Second Issue — 1972, 50th Anniversary Series	31
	CT22-1 Lined Counters in Tinted Counter Blocks	32
	CT22-2 Black Counters in Tinted Counter Blacks	33
CT23	Third Issue — 1974, Triangle Logo Design	35
CT24	Fourth Issue — 1976, Montreal "Olympiade XXI Olympiad"	40
CT25	Fifth Issue — 1985, Modified Triangle Logo Design	43
	CT25-1 Large Red Serial Number - One Signature	44
	CT25-2 Small Red Serial Number - One Signature	45
	CT25-3 Small Red Serial Number - Two Signatures	46
CT26	Sixth Issue — 1987, Modified Triangle With Warning	48
	CT26-1 Small Red Seven Digit Serial Number	49
	CT26-2 Small Red Eight Digit Serial Number	51
	CT26-3 Small Red Ten Digit Serial Number	53
CT27	Seventh Issue — 1989, Modified Triangle with Warning	54
	CT27-1 Large Red Seven Digit Serial Number	55
	CT27-2 Large Black Seven Digit Serial Number	56
CT28	Eighth Issue — 1992, Large Sandy McTire Design	57
	CT28-1 Pasternak/Macaulay Signatures	58
	CT28-2 Kishner/Macaulay Signatures	60
	CT28-3 Pasternak/Bachand Signatures	61

INTRODUCTION

CANADIAN TIRE CORPORATION

The Canadian Tire Corporation is the principal wholesale supplier of merchandise to franchised Associate retail stores. These stores are operated by associate dealers who sell an extensive range of automotive parts and accessories, hardware and household goods. The Associate stores often operate service facilities including lubrication. The parent company operates a gas bar and Pit Stop at many Associate stores.

COMPANY HISTORY

The Hamilton Garage and Rubber Co. was a small one-bay, Ford, automobile service garage established at the corner of Gerrard and Hamilton Streets, Toronto, in 1909. John William Billes was appointed sales manager in 1913. In 1922 he purchased the business for $1,500.

John's younger brother, Alfred Jackson Billes, joined the business and the name of the firm was changed, September 15, 1922, to the Hamilton Tire and Rubber Co. The business was incorporated under Ontario charter, December 1, 1927, with the new name - Canadian Tire Corporation. John W. Billes was President and Alfred J. looked after the technical side of the business.

In 1923 the store was moved to the corner of Elm and Yonge Streets and in 1927 to the north-east corner of Yonge and Isabella Sts., Toronto. The address was 637 Yonge St. The company remained here until 1937 when it was moved to the north-east corner of Church and Yonge at 837 Yonge St.

The company issued their first road map in 1926 and their first direct sales catalogue in 1928. Billes franchised the first Associate store in 1934 when it was opened in Hamilton. A second was opened in Ottawa the same year. A franchise only required an investment of $1,500 and a store of 300 square feet. By 1974 over 20,000 square feet of display area was required for a franchise. By 1939 there were 71 Associate Stores. Progress was rapid with 108 Associate stores in 1941, 116 by 1946, 156 by 1956, 225 by 1966, and 269 stores and 49 gas bars in 1972.

By 1988 the corporation supported 404 Associate stores and 132 gas bars from coast to coast. The company had entered Quebec in the early 1950's to be followed by the Maritimes in that decade. Stores were established in Manitoba in 1966, Saskatchewan in 1972, Alberta in 1975 and British Columbia in 1980. The first gas bar was opened at the Yonge St. store in Toronto in the Fall of 1958. In 1973 the company's head office was moved to the Canada Square Building at Yonge and Eglinton Streets, Toronto.

By 1993 there were 424 Associate stores and 213 gas outlets across Canada. Several warehouse-style stores had been opened. The product line was expanded and the ratio of sales floor area to storage area had increased from 40:60 to 80:20 meaning more goods were on the sales floor than in storage.

John W. Billes died November 16, 1956, aged 60, and Alfred Billes, 54, became President. He introduced gas bars to the franchise operation. A new warehouse was built near Highway 401.

Alfred J. Billes retired as President in 1966. Vice President Joseph Dean Muncaster, 32, became Chief Executive Officer in the Spring of 1966. Muncaster had been with the company since 1957 as a financial analyst. Alex. E. Barron was Chairman of the Board.

The corporation underwent severe internal problems from 1983 to 1987 during a rearrangement of corporate ownership. Muncaster and Barron left the Company in May 1985. There was no Chief Executive Officer for 10 months.

In mid January 1986 new officers appointed included Dean Groussman as President and Chief Executive Officer, and Douglas H. Heuman as Vice President and Treasurer. Hugh Macaulay became Chairman of the Board replacing the late Alex Barron.

On August 1, 1992, Dean Groussman returned to the Zale Corporation of Dallas, Texas after seven years with Canadian Tire. The company was again left without a Chief Executive Officer.

Stanley W. Pasternak became Vice President and Treasurer. Gerald S. (Gerry) Kishner was appointed Executive Vice President, Finance, and Chief Financial Officer in 1989.

Stephen E. Bachand, formerly with Hechinger Co. of Landover, Maryland, was appointed President and Chief Executive Officer effective March 1, 1993.

COMPANY LOGO

In 1929 the triangle was adopted for the sale of a particular brand of oil. In 1933 the maple leaf in a circle appeared on the company road map for the year and in 1935 both the triangle and the maple leaf were included in an ad for Mor-Power batteries. The quality label (Proven Tested Products) was also adopted in 1935. The Superlastic trademark was instituted in 1928 and comprised a tire with legs and a silver dollar with legs as seen on this 1935 envelope.

Finally, an early version of the present triangle appeared in 1943. The corporation's three-sided logo is said to represent the Billes family, the Associate Dealers, and the public. In 1967 the logo was rejuvenated by Rich Hub and Bernie Freedman. The triangle was widened and the letter style opened up, the corners were rounded and the "red" colour was standardized to appeal to both male and female customers. The shape of the maple leaf became that of the new Canadian flag on signs. The name CANADIAN TIRE was made in a straight line rather than curved.

It has been pointed out that a triangle standing on its apex is unstable!

In 1941 a Scotsman, the forerunner of Sandy McTire, appeared as a caddy on the company catalogue. He seemed to win over his two sons. In 1944 a girl was added to the design. Muncaster phased out these interesting catalogue covers, the last design was in 1971. The frugal happy Scot continues to be used on company coupons.

CASH BONUS COUPONS

Canadian Tire Corporation cash bonus coupons are the longest running series of modern merchant scrip in Canada. The Associate Stores which are dealer-operated and mainly dealer-owned, are allied with Canadian Tire Corporation by franchise agreements. The Corporation operates a wholesale organization to provide the Associate Store with products they sell.

Cash bonus coupons were originally issued at the corporation gas bars to promote the purchase of gasoline, and to retain the customers. The coupons are now only redeemable at the Associate store.

Cash bonus store coupons are used at participating stores for over-the-counter cash purchases, but not for service or labour charges. Cash bonus coupons are redeemable only at Canadian Tire Associate stores and only in association with consumer purchases of merchandise or Auto Centre service. The coupon bonus rate varies and in recent years is used as a freight equalizer. The bonus is 5% in the Toronto area, 4% in most of Ontario, and 3% in Quebec, Northern Ontario west to Thunder Bay and Nipigon, and the Maritimes except Newfoundland. Coupons are not issued in Western Canada although they are accepted in exchange for merchandise. Store coupons are not used in other areas. About $30 million of coupons are issued or replaced each year. Associate stores purchase the coupons from the company at face value and own them. Originally the coupon service was handled by the

Adjustment Department, with distribution being handled by the bank note company. As the volume increased a separate Coupon Department was established.

"Coin World" (June 1, 1962) described the origin of the coupons. Billes compared them to the store tokens of the 19th Century. Cash and credit customers were each receiving the same service and goods. The coupons were a discount for paying cash and they were a formal recognition of the fact rather than a simple reduction in price at the cash register. Billes considered them to be promissory notes. Since the coupons were to have the same recognition as cash the company decided they should have the appearance and feel as well. The British American Bank Note Company was commissioned to design and produce the Cash Bonus Discount Coupons for the gas bars, and to control counterfeiting.

The Cash Bonus Discount Coupons were first introduced to the public in late November 1958, when the first "gas bar" was opened at Yonge and Church St., Toronto, next to the main store. It had 5 pumps selling unbranded (Texaco) gasoline and a "lub" bay. Instead of participating in the many gas wars of the time the company held the price of gasoline at the standard rate for the area but gave coupons as an incentive to buy at the gas bars. The price of gasoline in 1958 was about 39.9 cents a gallon. The company discount varied from 5% to a high of 25%.

In 1960 a second gas bar was built on O'Connor Drive. This bar sold more gasoline "than any other in the world." The "put a tiger in your tank" giveaway by Imperial Oil started in 1960 and in June 1960 the supply of gasoline to CTC was cut off. The company threatened to buy 60 million gallons from the USSR. In October 1961 CTC was offering a 10 percent discount on regular grade gasoline by providing coupons for cross merchandising in its store. In December 1962 Imperial Oil again led the war against discounting. CTC had reduced their coupon to 7 percent, from 10 percent. It had been as high as 15 percent. Imperial Oil wanted it set at 5 percent which they felt was equivalent to the other services they offered. These frequent gas wars were the source of several CTC discount coupons, often called Gas War Bonds, said to be based on A.J.'s wife seeing Italian money.

The Simard family opened their first Canadian Tire store May 14, 1955, at 200 Dorchester St., Quebec, and issued gas bar coupons inscribed P. SIMARD INC. In 1972 the company printed coupons "Les Huiles Montcalm Inc." redeemable in merchandise in their Canadian Tire Store. Coupons were issued in denominations of 3¢, 5¢, 10¢, 25¢, $1.00 and $2.00. There were four series of coupons before they were discontinued in 1987.

Cash Bonus Store Coupons are first mentioned in the Fall/Winter catalogue of 1961-62 confirming they were available in 1961. There was not the urgency to start the 5% discount system as at the gas bars. A.J. Brown was in charge of introducing the system to the dealer organization. There was some reluctance to adopt the coupon system since the store cash registers had no space for coupons.

Coupons are first mentioned in the 1969 Annual Report of the Corporation on the Consolidated Balance Sheet. Under Liabilities and Shareholder Equity - Current Liabilities. There is a line item entitled Accrued Liabilities and Coupons Outstanding. In 1968 the amount was $9,821,341, it was $40,659,000 in 1978 and $134,544,000 in 1988. It is thought that coupons are a high percentage of this liability and show their rapid growth.

Both of the coupon series were designed by Bernie Freedman, project manager, Art and Display Department. Store coupons were redeemable at both the store for merchandise or at the gas bar. Store coupons were printed by the Canadian Bank Note Company.

When the original gas coupons were ready for printing in 1958 the Treasurer, Fred Sasaki was unavailable and the printer signed his name, unfortunately he spelled it "Saski". The same error was repeated in 1961 for the first issue of store coupons.

Denominations no longer in use, worn and misprinted coupons, are withdrawn from circulation by Associate stores and returned to the company for credit. In 1985 about 20 million coupons were placed in circulation. The redemption rate of store coupons is over 85 percent, less for gas bar coupons.

In April 1992 the company began to consolidate the gas bar and store coupons. A new coupon design was selected to supersede existing coupons in circulation. Old series were withdrawn.

PRINTING SEQUENCE

The method of printing affects the appearance of the coupon and creates minor varieties. From an examination of coupons, it appears that the basic design for a series is printed in black (including density or shades) on white bank note rag paper having security planchets. The red serial number is printed on the note during this sequence. (See below for example of the single printing).

The second operation prints the background colour for that coupon as well as the coupon value. In many coupons there are minor and major differences in registration causing the coupon value to be high, low, left or right in the coupon box. (See below for example) Coupons also exist where the back has not been printed and with other flaws which escaped inspection. The coupon is one colour but the density changes. There are many shades of colour.

GRADING

When grading a coupon it is essential to first determine if the coupon may be safely removed from its holder without causing any damage due to brittleness, unseen tears, glue remnants, etc. Then, carefully remove the coupon and holding it lightly, consider the general appearance, amount of wear, the hue and intensity of the colour of both the face and back. Determine a preliminary grade. If the coupon is Fine or better it should be held obliquely in line with a good light source. Move it around at various angles, such that the light will reflect off the coupon highlighting any ripples, counting creases, heavy creases, pressed out creases, tears, pinholes, cancellations, repairs or fading. The mastering of this technique is mandatory in successfully grading coupons. When these have been carefully considered, one must decide if these are "normal" for the preliminary grade which was determined. If not, then the grade may have to be reduced depending on the number and severity of the defects, or the defects will have to be listed in addition to the overall grade, followed by any unusual defect, than to down grade the coupon.

To accurately grade a coupon it is also necessary to consider any additional impairments. These may include:

1. Minor counting creases or edge defects, especially for UNC and EF grades.
2. Tears, pinholes or signature perforations.
3. Stains, smudges, crayon marks or writing.
4. Missing corners, cut and punch cancellations or edge defects.
5. Undesirable rubber stamps.
6. Any repairs, such as with sticky tape, scotch tape, stamp hinges, etc.
7. Chemical damage, paste or glue from attachment to a page.
8. Poorly centered or badly trimmed edges.

UNCIRCULATED (UNC.) - A perfect coupon. Crisp and clean as when printed and without any creases or pinholes. Colours have original hue and intensity.

ABOUT UNCIRCULATED (AU) - Similar to Uncirculated, but it will have either a very light fold or ripple "counting creases," to the extent that the paper fibers are not broken. If any combination of the two are present, the coupon would fall into the extremely fine grade.

It has been common practice, by some, to add a "plus", "+", "about" or "almost" to infer a slightly higher or lower condition than the designated grade. Eg. about VF, VF+, almost EF.

EXTREMELY FINE (EF) - Very crisp, clean and colourful as an uncirculated coupon, but has a major crease or several minor creases. The coupon may or may not show some slight evidence of wear.

VERY FINE (VF) - A fairly crisp and clean coupon. It may have several major and minor creases and folds, some evidence of wear especially along the edges or at the corners. There may be some slight decrease in hue and intensity of the colours. The design in the creases should not be worn off.

FINE (F) - A coupon with considerable evidence of circulation. Numerous creases and folds, but a small degree of firmness remaining. Usually fairly soiled and the hue and intensity of the colour are slightly reduced. There may be a slight amount of the design worn off along the major creases.

VERY GOOD (VG) - A heavily circulated coupon but with all the major design still visible. Usually limp with no crispness or firmness, quite soiled, hue and intensity of the colour will be faded or altered. A moderate amount of the design may be worn off along the major creases or in the "counting crease" areas. Numerous other defects may apply (see list above).

GOOD (G) - Similar to VG, but often with tears and small pieces missing. Usually some of the major design is worn off. Signatures are often unreadable. The coupon is very limp and usually has numerous other defects.

FAIR (F) - Similar to Good, but larger pieces missing. Signatures and sheet numbers entirely missing. Often has numerous tears and other defects.

POOR (P) - As a Fair coupon, but with a major portion of the coupon torn off or the design obliterated. Often numerous tape repairs. Generally collectable only because of rarity.

Careful inspection to determine the correct grade will lead to greater trust and confidence between buyers and sellers of coupons.

SPECIMEN COUPONS

Specimen coupons are not intended for circulation and are not redeemable. Specimen coupons are produced by companies to show employees their appearance so that they may be recognized. They are also used for promotional purposes. Most are stamped SPECIMEN and are perforated, called punch cancelling, through the signature area. Specimen coupons have a prefix letter followed by zeros. Some Canadian Tire specimen coupons are uniface.

Proof, specimen and essay coupons are commonly accepted as being in uncirculated condition, otherwise, they should be described as impaired with the type and degree of impairment stated.

REPLACEMENT COUPONS

Replacement coupons (A) are specifically printed to replace coupons that are spoiled during the manufacturing process to keep the total count correct. Several devices are used to identify such coupons. The British American Bank Note Company replaced damaged coupons with another having the same prefix and serial number. These are very difficult to differentiate from other coupons. The Canadian Bank Note Company usually used an asterisk before or after the prefix to indicate a replacement coupon. A special serial number was also used.

SPECIAL NUMBER COUPONS

Collectors frequently collect special number coupons and are willing to pay a modest premium to acquire one. A radar coupon is one with a palindromic sheet number. This number portion of the serial number reads the same backwards as forwards. The scarcity of the radar increases as the number of digits decrease, ie, a solid number being the rarest. Examples of special number coupons, with a 7 - digit serial number, are ordinary radar: 9655569; solid radar coupons: 1111111; million coupons: 5000000; six-digit repeater: 3 111 111; two digit radar: 1000001 or 3344433: ladder: 2345678 or 0987654; also low serial numbers 0000001.

NUMBERING SYSTEM

We have revised the numbering system for the second edition, hopefully for the better. From experience we have found that systems seem to evolve over time and after three or four editions we end up with one that is workable. It is nigh on impossible to conceive a numbering system out of the blue with so many variables, both minor and major, to consider. Something new always surfaces making adjustments mandatory.

Gas Bar Coupons are numbered CT1 to CT3 leaving a gap in the numbers to CT21 which is the beginning of the Store Coupon numbers. The reason for this gap is to allow for the possible expansion of the gas bar coupon series. The last whole number 1, 2, etc, signifies the issue number of either the gas bar or store coupon. The next classification, major variety of the issue, is by a hyphenated whole number.

Example: CT2-1: "1" being the first major variety.

The letters following the major variety classification are for minor varieties. They signify the following:

a: Four digit serial number
b: Five digit serial number
c: Six digit serial number
d: Seven digit serial number
e: Eight digit serial number
SP: Specimen note
R: Replacement note

and then A, B, C etc, as is indicated by the minor variety section within the major variety category.

GAS BAR COUPONS
CT1 to CT3

Canadian Tire Corporation opened their first Mor Power Service Station to sell gasoline in 1957. A state of the art lubritorium was added in mid November 1958 at 745 Yonge St., Toronto. It was a gas bar and lubritorium. The "Rural Scene" discount coupons were originally used at this gas bar.

CT1   **FIRST ISSUE — 1958**
              RURAL SCENE WITH CTC STORE

Black Counters in Tinted Counter Blocks
Single Serial Number in Red

Face:

CT1-5: Security frame with SAVE SAFELY at left and EPARGNES ASSURES at right. The imprint BRITISH AMERICAN BANK NOTE COMPANY LIMITED is at the bottom. Background is white paper with dense pattern of "cTc" in a maple leaf. The density of the colour varies. On the background the company quality seal - a maple leaf with cTc within a ribbon circle bearing the words TESTED PROVEN PRODUCTS. To left, a running tire with happy face, and a running dollar sign, a symbol used by the company for many years. CANADIAN TIRE \ CORPORATION LIMITED \ value in English and in French. A lined black rectangle bearing the words WE MAKE YOUR DOLLARS GO FARTHER. Below, in English at left and French at right, REDEEMABLE IN MERCHANDISE \ AT CANADIAN TIRE STORES, and, REMBOURSABLE EN MARCHANDISE \ AUX MAGASINS CANADIAN TIRE. The coupon counter, or value, is in tall thin numerals in each corner of the coupon. The serial number has a prefix letter and five or six digits, in red, and is above the company name. The coupon is lithographed, not engraved, on heavy paper.

Back:

CT1-5: In the security frame the words WE MAKE YOUR DOLLARS GO FARTHER, SAVE SAFELY, EPARGNES ASSURES and CANADIAN TIRE CORPORATION LIMITED. A composite scene depicting wheat fields, oil wells, factory, transportation, and featuring a Canadian Tire Associate store and sun bearing the words TESTED PROVEN. The values are not in boxes.

SPECIMEN COUPONS

Specimen coupons exist for each denomination in this issue. The word SPECIMEN in large outlined red serifed letters is at an angle on the front and back of the coupon. The serial number is omitted and the coupons are perforated through the signatures.

Face:
CT1-5SP

Back:
CT1-5SP

Signatures: F. Saski, Treasurer and A. Billes, President
The spelling of "Sasaki" is in error on the first issue.
Imprint: British American Bank Note Company Limited

Serial Number:

CT1-2b (Five digits)

CT1-2C (Six digits)

Prefix letter with five or six digits in red. Specimen coupons have no serial number. The serial numbers of CT1 cross-over and continue into CT5 about:

A Prefix - 3,000,000 C Prefix - 340,000
B Prefix -   560,000 D Prefix -   55,000

TECHNICAL DATA

Cat.No.	Coupon Value	Coupon Colour	Serial Number Low	Serial Number Est. Low	Serial Number High	Estimate of Quantity Printed
CT1-1b	5¢	Green	A00450	A00001	A96812	100,000
CT1-1c	5¢	Green	A143719	A100000	A180749	81,000
CT1-1SP	5¢	Green				Unknown
CT1-2b	10¢	Rose	B02106	B00001	B21856	100,000
CT1-2c	10¢	Rose	B152015	B100000	B552445	453,000
CT1-2SP	10¢	Rose				Unknown
CT1-3b	25¢	Violet	C09051	C00001	C88242	100,000
CT1-3c	25¢	Violet	C122572	C100000	C337244	238,000
CT1-3SP	25¢	Violet				Unknown
CT1-4b	50¢	Orange	D06383	D00001	D50713	51,000
CT1-4SP	50¢	Orange				Unknown
CT1-5b	$1.00	Brown	E00014	E00001	E15990	61,000
CT1-5SP	$1.00	Brown				Unknown

PRICING TABLE

Cat.No.	Coupon Value	Serial Number Prefix	Serial Number Digits	Coupon Colour	F	VF	Unc
CT1-1b	5¢	A	5	Green	20.00	35.00	100.00
CT1-1c	5¢	A	6	Green	25.00	45.00	125.00
CT1-1SP	5¢	-	-	Green	Specimen		100.00
CT1-2b	10¢	B	5	Rose	20.00	35.00	100.00
CT1-2c	10¢	B	6	Rose	15.00	25.00	75.00
CT1-2SP	10¢	-	-	Rose	Specimen		100.00
CT1-3b	25¢	C	5	Violet	25.00	40.00	125.00
CT1-3c	25¢	C	6	Violet	20.00	30.00	80.00
CT1-3SP	25¢	-	-	Violet	Specimen		100.00
CT1-4b	50¢	D	5	Orange	40.00	100.00	200.00
CT1-4SP	50¢	-	-	Orange	Specimen		100.00
CT1-5b	$1.00	E	5	Brown	15.00	25.00	100.00
CT1-5SP	$1.00	-	-	Brown	Specimen		100.00

CT2 SECOND ISSUE — 1961
MAP OF CANADA WITH GAS BAR & CTC STORE

Tinted Counters in Black Counter Blocks

This series was printed by the Advertising and Sales Promotion Department on a glossy grade of paper at the Sheppard Warehouse Distribution Centre. The design is coarse and the serial numbers tend to be uneven. The serial numbering unit is 25 mm overall. It consists of a letter and space for seven numerals. When only four, five or six numerals are used there is additional space between the letter and the first numeral. Note size (printed area) is 122 mm long and 64 mm high. The 1¢ coupon has CASH BONUS in the upper security frame on the back.

Face:

CT2-4: The second issue is similar to CT3-1 except the security frame does not bear the printers name, the seal has been replaced by the lined company triangle logo, there are two serial numbers that are below the company name, and the coupon value is in the background colour in black boxes. The density of colour ranges from yellow orange to bright orange. The values are not written on the face of the coupon.

Back:

CT2-4: Security frame with CUSTOMER PROFIT SHARING BONUS at bottom. The background pattern is the same as on the front. The central motif is a semi circle with DEDICATED TO CANADIAN GROWTH above. Within the semi circle, in black, a map of Canada, the cTc logo, and the original Associate store located at the north-west corner of Dunlop and High Streets in Barrie. The gas bar sign reads MOR POWER GAS. Values are in each corner in large numerals within a black rectangle. The 1¢ coupon has CASH BONUS in the upper security frame. The same back was used for CT-3.

Signatures: F. Sasaki, Treasurer and A. Billes, President
Imprint: None. The BRITISH AMERICAN BANK NOTE COMPANY LIMITED imprint was removed from the bottom of the security frame on the original face plate, a lighter area indicates where the words were removed.

CT2-1 Two Serial Numbers in Red

Face:
CT2-1-4c

Serial Number: Prefix letter and six digits printed in red.

TECHNICAL DATA

Cat.No.	Coupon Value	Serial No. Colour	Serial Number Low	Est. Low	High	Estimate of Quantity Printed
CT2-1-1c	1¢	Red	Z054211	Z000001	Z341235	342,000
CT2-1-2c	2¢	Red	Y044424	Y000001	Y563458	564,000
CT2-1-3c	3¢	Red	X002595	X000001	X515097	516,000
CT2-1-4c	3¢	Red	Z107051	Z000001	Z162763	163,000
CT2-1-5c	4¢	Red	W021709	W000001	W507059	510,000

PRICING TABLE

Cat.No.	Coupon Value	Serial Number Prefix	Digits	Serial No. Colour	F	VF	Unc
CT2-1-1c	1¢	Z	6	Red	6.00	10.00	30.00
CT2-1-2c	2¢	Y	6	Red	8.00	15.00	40.00
CT2-1-3c	3¢	X	6	Red	6.00	10.00	30.00
CT2-1-4c	3¢	Z	6	Red	8.00	15.00	40.00
CT2-1-5c	4¢	W	6	Red	10.00	20.00	50.00

CT2-2   One Serial Number in Red or Black

Face:
CT2-2-11c

Serial Number: One prefix letter with four, five or six digits in red or black.

TECHNICAL DATA

Cat.No.	Coupon Value	Serial No. Colour	Low	Serial Number Est. Low	High	Estimate of Quantity Printed
CT2-2-1b	1¢	Red	A20093	A00001	A99361	100,000
CT2-2-1bB	1¢	Red	A41557	A41000	A42245	1,250
CT2-2-2c	1¢	Red	A100225	A100000	A100725	800
CT2-2-3c	1¢	Black	E 010401	E000001	E213882	215,000
CT2-2-4a	2¢	Red	B4253	B0001	B9784	10,000
CT2-2-5b	2¢	Red	B53940	B10000	B65218	55,000
CT2-2-6c	2¢	Black	E028927	E000001	E039533	40,000
CT2-2-7c	2¢	Black	F000032	F000001	F078448	80,000
CT2-2-8c	2¢	Red	Y577466	Y565000	Y614769	45,000
CT2-2-9a	3¢	Red	C2287	C0001	C7154	10,000
CT2-2-10b	3¢	Red	C17792	C10000	C98885	90,000
CT2-2-11c	3¢	Red	C101766	C100000	C357851	168,000
CT2-2-11cA	3¢	Red	C262493	C260000	C353397	90,000
CT2-2-12bA	3¢	Black	X01122	X0001	X87814	100,000
CT2-2-13c	3¢	Red	X518649	X515000	X617490	100,000
CT2-2-13cA	3¢	Black	X000840	X000001	X998156	1,000,000
CT2-2-14bA	3¢	Black	Y00467	Y00001	Y98066	100,000
CT2-2-15cA	3¢	Black	Y105526	Y100001	Y119662	20,000
CT2-2-16c	4¢	Red	W514133	W510000	W521094	10,000
CT2-2-17c	4¢	Red	Y 534711		Unknown	

Varieties:

With "Mor Power"

"Mor Power" Omitted

A. MOR POWER omitted from store company sign. Coupons CT2-2-9e to CT2-2-11cA, CT2-2-12bA, C2-2-13cA, CT2-2-14bA and CT2-2-1-15cA have MOR POWER omitted.

Without "No."

With "No."

B. 1¢ Coupon has 'No.' added to prefix letters.

C. A 3¢ coupon with a single black prefix "W" exists in this series. It bears the Sasaki-Muncaster signatures. The "W" is very large and heavy sans-serif, the digits are small and light and are not part of the series. It is printed on thin letter paper. Only one coupon is known to exist and thus is not listed.

PRICING TABLE

Cat.No.	Coupon Value	Serial Number Prefix	Serial Number Digit	Serial Colour	F	VF	Unc
CT2-2-1b	1¢	A	5	Red	5.00	8.00	20.00
CT2-2-1bB	1¢	A No.	5	Red	8.00	15.00	35.00
CT2-2-2c	1¢	A	6	Red	20.00	35.00	100.00
CT2-2-3c	1¢	E	6	Black	6.00	10.00	30.00
CT2-2-4a	2¢	B	4	Red	5.00	8.00	20.00
CT2-2-5b	2¢	B	5	Red	8.00	15.00	35.00
CT2-2-6c	2¢	E	6	Black	5.00	10.00	25.00
CT2-2-7c	2¢	F	6	Black	5.00	8.00	20.00
CT2-2-8c	2¢	Y	6	Red	5.00	10.00	25.00
CT2-2-9a	3¢	C	4	Red	6.00	10.00	30.00
CT2-2-10b	3¢	C	5	Red	5.00	8.00	20.00
CT2-2-11c	3¢	C	6	Red	15.00	25.00	60.00
CT2-2-11cA	3¢	C	6	Red	15.00	25.00	60.00
CT2-2-12bA	3¢	X	5	Black	5.00	8.00	20.00
CT2-2-13c	3¢	X	6	Red	15.00	30.00	75.00
CT2-2-13cA	3¢	X	6	Black	15.00	25.00	60.00
CT2-2-14bA	3¢	Y	5	Black	5.00	8.00	20.00
CT2-2-15cA	3¢	Y	6	Black	5.00	10.00	25.00
CT2-2-16c	4¢	W	6	Red	10.00	20.00	50.00
CT2-2-17c	4¢	Y	6	Red	15.00	25.00	60.00

CT2-3   No Serial Number on Face or Back

Face:
CT2-3-11

Serial Number: No serial number

Varieties:

    A. MOR POWER omitted. About 37% of the 3¢ coupons have MOR POWER omitted. See photograph under varieties on page no. 8 for an illustration of this variety.

TECHNICAL DATA

Cat.No.	Coupon Value	Coupon Colour	Serial Number Low	Est. Low	High	Estimate of Quantity Printed
CT2-3-1	3¢	Orange		No Serial Number		Unknown
CT2-3-1A	3¢	Orange		No Serial Number		Unknown

PRICING TABLE

Cat.No.	Coupon Value	Serial Number	Coupon Colour	F	VF	Unc
CT2-3-1	3¢	None	Orange	3.00	6.00	15.00
CT2-3-1A	3¢	None	Orange	4.00	7.00	20.00

CT3 THIRD ISSUE — 1961
MODIFIED MAP OF CANADA

The original Rural Scene CT-1 series had five denominations. When the series was redesigned with a centre serial number in 1961 it continued the six digit serial numbers of the Rural Scene. The $1.00 coupon was not printed as this coupon had small circulation and there was a sufficient stock of Rural Scene coupons available. When the 6-digit serial numbers were exhausted in some denominations a 7-digit serial number followed. For those series where the serial number was still less than 999999 a "0" was added to make it a 7-digit serial number. About 1964 the Petroleum Division thought the series was not flexible enough and extra denominations were created. The 11 denominations proved not to be a good answer to control the problem and by 1977 gas bar cashiers had only a few coupons over 35¢.

Black Counters in Tinted Counter Blocks

Face:

CT3-1-2c: A lined security frame with SAVE SAFELY at left and ECONOMIE! SECURITE! at right. The name BRITISH AMERICAN BANK NOTE COMPANY LIMITED is in the lower frame. The corporation name CANADIAN TIRE/CORPORATION LIMITED in two lines upon a lined triangle with maple leaf and cTc above. At left, a running tire and dollar on a double lined rectangle bearing the words WE MAKE YOUR DOLLARS GO FARTHER. Below the rectangle the statement REDEEMABLE IN MERCHANDISE/AT CANADIAN TIRE STORES, and, REMBOURSABLE EN MARCHANDISE/AUX MAGASINS CANADIAN TIRE. The values are tall slim numerals, in black, in rectangles at each corner having the background colour of the coupon. The coupon is engraved and the background colour is formed by many "cTc" within a circle. The serial number, in red, is below the corporation name in the centre of the coupon.

Back:

CT3-1-2c: The words CUSTOMER PROFIT SHARING BONUS on the lower portion of a double lined security frame. A portion of a globe showing a map of Canada upon which is superimposed a Canadian Tire Associate Store and Mor-Power Gas Bar, with the corporation triangle. Lines radiate from the globe. DEDICATED TO CANADIAN GROWTH is above the globe. Values are unboxed in each corner. Imprint below the design reads BRITISH AMERICAN BANK NOTE COMPANY LIMITED OTTAWA.

SPECIMEN COUPONS

Face:
CT3-1-1SP

Back:

CT3-1-1SP Specimen coupons exist for each denomination in this issue. The word SPECIMEN is printed in red across the face of the coupon above the logo. The serial number has a prefix letter A with zeros. The coupon is punched cancelled at the signatures. The back has a black control number.

CT3-1 Centre Serial Number in Red
Below Corporate Name

In 1964 six new denominations, 15¢, 20¢, 30¢, 35¢, 40¢, 45¢, and 60¢, were created and added to the series.

Face:
CT3-1-6dA

12

Signatures: F. Sasaki, Treasurer and A Billes, President

Serial Number: One prefix letter with six or seven digits in red.

    CT3-1-2c Six Digits   CT3-5-1-2d Seven Digits

Cross-over serial numbers have seven digits. The seven digit numbers of CT3-1-2d continue into CT3-2. Cross over serial numbers are estimated to be:

A - 1902500	B - 3353000	C - 1560000
E - 0125000	F - 0290000	G - 0240000
H - 0170000	L - 0150000	J - 0236000
K - 0200000	M - 0300000	

TECHNICAL DATA

Cat.No.	Coupon Value	Coupon Colour	Serial Number Low	Serial Number Est. Low	Serial Number High	Estimate of Quantity Printed
CT3-1-1c	5¢	Green	A318626	A181000	A998494	800,000
CT3-1-1cSP	5¢	Green	A000000			Unknown
CT3-1-1d	5¢	Green	A1012239	A1000000	A1900739	900,000
CT3-1-2c	10¢	Red	B583909	B553000	B991449	450,000
CT3-1-2cSP	10¢	Red	B000000			Unknown
CT3-1-2d	10¢	Red	B1115765	B1000000	B3352350	2,350,000
CT3-1-3d	15¢	Green	E0000236	E0000001	E0123435	125,000
CT3-1-4d	20¢	Green	F0003247	F0000001	F0285461	290,000
CT3-1-5c	25¢	Violet	C346830	C338000	C993224	660,000
CT3-1-5cSP	25¢	Violet	C000000			Unknown
CT3-1-5d	25¢	Violet	C1016679	C1000000	C1554576	560,000
CT3-1-6d	30¢	Green	G0002402	G0000001	G0139999	140,000
CT3-1-6dA	30¢	Green	-	G0140000	G0233184	100,000
CT3-1-7d	35¢	Green	H0012991	H0000001	H0167702	175,000
CT3-1-8d	40¢	Green	J0001074	J0000001	J0235733	236,000
CT3-1-9d	45¢	Green	K0003333	K0000001	K0214435	215,000
CT3-1-10c	50¢	Brown	D059764	D051000	D654723	600,000
CT3-1-10ScP	50¢	Brown	D000000			Unknown
CT3-1-11d	50¢	Green	M0003592	M0000001	M0296554	300,000
CT3-1-12d	60¢	Green	L0000081	L0000001	L0161612	100,000
CT3-1-12dA	60¢	Green	-	L0100000	L0161612	70,000

Imprint:
Face: British American Bank Note Company Limited
Back: British American Bank Note Company Limited Ottawa

Varieties:

CT3-1-5 Heavy Type Font

CT3-1--6 Light Type Font

A. The type font used for the value in CT3-1 is heavier than that used for CT3-2. In the CT3-1-5 series the 30¢ and 60¢ coupons exist with the lighter CT3-2 font type. These are CT3-1-5-6dA and CT3-1-5-12dA in the pricing chart below.

PRICING TABLE

Cat.No.	Coupon Value	Serial Number Prefix	Digit	Coupon Colour	F	VF	Unc
CT3-1-1c	5¢	A	6	Green	4.00	10.00	20.00
CT3-1-1cSP	5¢	A	6	Green	Specimen		100.00
CT3-1-1d	5¢	A	7	Green	4.00	8.00	20.00
CT3-1-2c	10¢	B	6	Red	3.00	5.00	15.00
CT3-1-2cSP	10¢	B	6	Red	Specimen		100.00
CT3-1-2d	10¢	B	7	Red	6.00	12.00	30.00
CT3-1-3d	15¢	E	7	Green	15.00	25.00	60.00
CT3-1-4d	20¢	F	7	Green	10.00	20.00	50.00
CT3-1-5c	25¢	C	6	Violet	5.00	12.00	20.00
CT3-1-5cSP	25¢	C	6	Violet	Specimen		100.00
CT3-1-5d	25¢	C	7	Violet	5.00	10.00	25.00
CT3-1-6d	30¢	G	7	Green.	15.00	25.00	60.00
CT3-1-6dA	30¢	G	7	Green	15.00	30.00	65.00
CT3-1-7d	35¢	H	7	Green	10.00	20.00	50.00
CT3-1-8d	40¢	J	7	Green	10.00	20.00	50.00
CT3-1-9d	45¢	K	7	Green	10.00	20.00	50.00
CT3-1-10c	50¢	D	6	Brown	5.00	10.00	25.00
CT3-1-10cSP	50¢	-	6	Brown	Specimen		100.00
CT3-1-11d	50¢	M	7	Green	4.00	8.00	20.00
CT3-1-12d	60¢	L	7	Green	15.00	35.00	75.00
CT3-1-12dA	60¢	L	7	Green	20.00	40.00	80.00

CT3-2   Centre Serial Number In Red Above Corporate Name

Sasaki/Billes Signatures

Face:
CT3-2

Signatures: F. Sasaki, Treasurer and A Billes, President
Serial Number: One letter prefix with seven digits in red.

TECHNICAL DATA

Cat.No.	Coupon Value	Colour	Serial Number Low	Est. Low	High	Estimate of Quantity Printed
CT3-2-1	5¢	Green	A1903166	A1902000	A3449780	1,550,000
CT3-2-2	5¢	Green	S1001339	S0000001	S3986869	4,000,000
CT3-2-2A	5¢	Green	S4181615	S4000000	S4704007	700,000
CT3-2-2AB	5¢	Green		Included Above		
CT3-2-3	10¢	Green	B3353297	B3352500	B4700729	1,350,000
CT3-2-4	10¢	Green	T0017859	T0000001	T2480899	2,500,000
CT3-2-4A	10¢	Green	T2581530	T2500000	T3499507	1,000,000
CT3-2-5	10¢	Red	T3550346	T3500000	T6333294	2,800,000
CT3-2-5A	10¢	Red	T6451857	T6400000	T7506445	1,100,000
CT3-2-6	15¢	Green	E0129633	E0125000	E1906880	1,800,000
CT3-2-7	20¢	Green	F0290901	F0290000	F2337367	2,000,000
CT3-2-8	25¢	Green	C1563284	C1560000	C3010508	1,450,000
CT3-2-9A	25¢	Green	U0517928	U0500000	U0879036	380,000
CT3-2-10	25¢	Green	V0027134	V0000001	V0475995	475,000
CT3-2-10A	25¢	Green	V0890150	V0600000	V1791941	1,200,000
CT3-2-11	25¢	Violet	V1919059	V1800000	V4517798	2,700,000
CT3-2-11A	25¢	Violet	V4597592	V4500000	V4774969	275,000
CT3-2-12	30¢	Green	G0248822	G0240000	G1234509	1,000,000
CT3-2-13	35¢	Green	H0179443	H0170000	H0707563	600,000
CT3-2-14	40¢	Green	J0237113	J0236900	J1246313	1,000,000
CT3-2-15	45¢	Green	K0218528	K0216000	K03899597	180,000
CT3-2-16	50¢	Green	M0311419	M0300000	M1045342	700,000
CT3-2-17A	50¢	Green	U0004079	U0000001	U0447566	450,000
CT3-2-18	25¢	Brown	U0894689	U0600000	U4081058	3,500,000
CT3-2-18A	50¢	Brown	U4106037	U4100000	U4687676	590,000
CT3-2-19	60¢	Green	L0173158	L0170000	L0944199	775,000
CT3-2-20	$1.00	Green	Z0000250	Z0000001	Z0249968	250,000
CT3-2-21A	$1.00	Yellow	Z0261566	Z0250000	Z1341015	1,100,000

Imprint:
  Face: British American Bank Note Company Limited
  Back: British American Bank Note Company Limited Ottawa

Varieties:

CT3-2 Without Serifs

CT3-2-2A With Serifs

A. The serial number prefix letter with serifs.

CT3-2-2A Normal Serif "S"

CT3-2-2AB Inverted Serif "S"

B. CT3-2-2AB inverted "S" is an error variety in which the prefix serif "S" is inverted as shown above.

PRICING TABLE

Cat.No.	Coupon Value	Serial Prefix	Coupon Colour	F	VF	Unc
CT3-2-1	5¢	A	Green	5.00	10.00	25.00
CT3-2-2	5¢	S	Green	3.00	5.00	15.00
CT3-2-2A	5¢	S	Green	3.00	5.00	15.00
CT3-2-2AB	5¢	S	Green	5.00	8.00	25.00
CT3-2-3	10¢	B	Green	5.00	10.00	25.00
CT3-2-4	10¢	T	Green	6.00	10.00	30.00
CT3-2-4A	10¢	T	Green	2.00	4.00	10.00
CT3-2-5	10¢	T	Red	5.00	8.00	25.00
CT3-2-5A	10¢	T	Red	4.00	7.00	20.00
CT3-2-6	15¢	E	Green	4.00	8.00	20.00
CT3-2-7	20¢	F	Green	4.00	8.00	20.00
CT3-2-8	25¢	C	Green	5.00	10.00	25.00
CT3-2-9A	25¢	U	Green	10.00	20.00	50.00
CT3-2-10	25¢	V	Green	6.00	10.00	30.00
CT3-2-10A	25¢	V	Green	8.00	15.00	40.00
CT3-2-11	25¢	V	Violet	5.00	8.00	25.00
CT3-2-11A	25¢	V	Violet	10.00	20.00	50.00
CT3-2-12	30¢	G	Green	6.00	10.00	30.00
CT3-2-13	35¢	H	Green	8.00	15.00	40.00
CT3-2-14	40¢	J	Green	6.00	12.00	30.00
CT3-2-15	45¢	K	Green	15.00	30.00	60.00
CT3-2-16	50¢	M	Green	8.00	15.00	40.00
CT3-2-17A	50¢	U	Green	8.00	15.00	40.00
CT3-2-18	50¢	U	Brown	4.00	7.00	20.00
CT3-2-18A	50¢	U	Brown	5.00	8.00	25.00
CT3-2-19	60¢	L	Green	8.00	15.00	40.00
CT3-2-20	$1.00	Z	Green	10.00	20.00	50.00
CT3-2-21A	$1.00	Z	Yellow	6.00	10.00	30.00

CT3-3 Centre Serial Number in Red Above Corporate Name

Heuman/Groussman Signatures

This is the final issue for gas bar coupons. In 1992 the gas bar coupon series was withdrawn by the Corporation and was superseded by regular store coupons.

Face:
CT3-3-5

Signatures: Douglas Heuman, Treasurer and Dean Groussman, President
Imprint:
　Face: British American Bank Note Inc. Ottawa, Canada
　Back: British American Bank Note Company Limited Ottawa Canada
Serial Number: Prefix letter has serifs with seven digits
Varieties:
　　A. Inverted "S" type CT3-1A has the prefix "S" inverted. See CT3 for inverted "S" illustration.

TECHNICAL DATA

Cat.No.	Coupon Value	Coupon Colour	Serial Number Low	Serial Number Est. Low	Serial Number High	Estimate of Quantity Printed
CT3-3-1	5¢	Green	S14771333	S4750000	S8445881	3,800,000
CT3-3-1A	5¢	Green	Included above			
CT3-3-2	10¢	Red	T0512133	T0000001	T1989899	2,000,000
CT3-3-2	10¢	Red	T7029623	T7020000	T9220971	2,000,000
CT3-3-3	25¢	Violet	V4796060	V4750000	V6687081	1,500,000
CT3-3-4	50¢	Brown	U4765818	U4700000	U6768094	2,000,000
CT3-3-5	$1.00	Yellow	Z1353128	Z1350000	Z2442463	1,100,000

PRICING TABLE

Cat.No.	Coupon Value	Serial Prefix	Coupon Colour	F	VF	Unc
CT3-3-1	5¢	S	Green	1.00	2.00	5.00
CT3-3-1A	5¢	S	Green	2.00	5.00	20.00
CT3-3-2	10¢	T	Red	1.50	3.00	7.00
CT3-3-3	25¢	V	Violet	1.50	3.00	8.00
CT3-3-4	50¢	U	Brown	1.50	3.00	7.00
CT3-3-5	$1.00	Z	Yellow	2.00	4.00	10.00

MISCELLANEOUS
GAS BAR COUPONS
CTM1 to CTM5

These special coupons are from the Petroleum Division of the Corporation. They were issued to promote the sale of gasoline and petroleum products during the several gas wars that erupted in the early 1960's and '70's. The coupons have the appearance of good quality printing.

CTM1   "HERCULES" GAS WAR COUPON

The origin of this issue is well described in "Freewheeling" by Brown, at page 116. The coupons are offset printed on bond paper, probably by the Corporation's printing department in early 1964.

Face:

CTM1-3: A vignette at left illustrating "Hercules" astride several forms of energy delivery and swinging a spiked ball and chain. At right a Canadian Tire gas bar showing the gas pumps with BONUS COUPONS above and SAVE 8% below. The coupon value in white is in a black circle in the upper corners. The coupon carries the title in outline letters GAS WAR / SAVINGS COUPON / REDEMPTION DEFERRED - SEE REVERSE. Double serial numbers, in red, are at the bottom

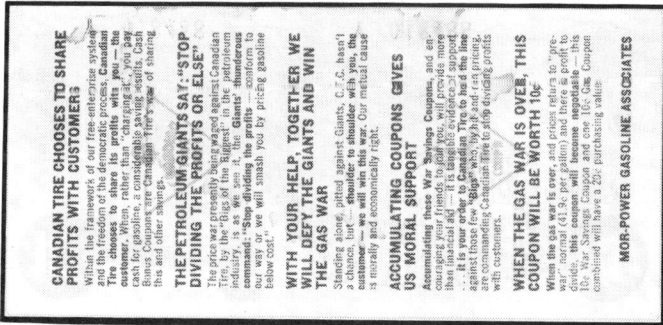

Back:

CTM1-3

The back carries a lengthy statement of Canadian Tire policy with regard to the gas war, the purpose of the coupon and the basis for its redemption. The final paragraph states that when the retail price of gasoline returns to 41.9¢ per gallon the coupon may be cashed in on the purchase of gasoline for its face value when accompanied with a regular 2¢ gasoline coupon (CT2-2) to double the coupon value. The 5¢, 10¢ and 25¢ coupons have higher redemption values. The credit line is MOR-POWER GASOLINE ASSOCIATES. The back of the coupon is white paper stock with a print colour the same as the face.

    Signatures: None
Serial Number: Prefix letter (no serifs) with six digit number.
      Imprint: None

PRICING TABLE

Cat. No.	Coupon Value	Prefix	Coupon Colour	Estimate Number	VF	Unc
CTM1-1	2¢	W	Gray black	175000	20.00	50.00
CTM1-2	5¢	X	Light green	65000	30.00	75.00
CTM1-3	10¢	Y	Orange	85000	30.00	75.00
CTM1-4	25¢	Z	Mauve	45000	40.00	100.00

CTM2   XV CENTS GAS WAR COUPON

In the Fall of 1964 Canadian Tire Corporation was the subject of a predatory price war organized by the Imperial Oil Co. who were squeezing the independant dealers. Imperial had guaranteed their dealers a commission of 5.5¢ to 7.5¢ per gallon regardless of the pump price. The price at CTC was 47.9¢ a gallon less 5 percent before the gas war.

On October 30, 1964, CTC sent a letter to dealers stating that one XV Gas War coupon was to be given with a $1.00 sale of gasoline. These coupons were used at the Toronto, Barrie and Quebec stores. A. J. Billes stated CTC could not compete due to small margins on gas sales so the coupon was to encourage customers to come back for a discount when margins were greater.

Face:

CTM2-1: A lined security frame with ECONOMIE! SECURITE! at left and SAVE SAFELY at right. CASH BONUS BON D'ACHAT is in the upper frame and CUSTOMER PROFIT SHARING BONUS is in the lower. At left is the Sandy McTire vignette. DISCOUNT 15¢ COUPON *SAVE 15¢ MAXIMUM ON EACH DOLLAR is in two lines upon a lined triangle with maple leaf and cTc above. Below is the redemption procedure: *ONE 15¢ COUPON REDUCES $1.00 PURCHASE TO 85¢ / FIVE 15¢ COUPONS REDUCE $5.25 PURCHASE TO $4.50 ETC. above a single-lined banner bearing the words APPLIES TO ALL CANADIAN TIRE CATALOGUED MERCHANDISE. Below the banner THAT PART OF SALE DISCOUNTED BY THIS COUPON IS / NOT SUBJECT TO CASH BONUS COUPONS / ISSUED BY AND REDEEMED ONLY AT / CANADIAN TIRE ASSOCIATE STORE - 839 YONGE, TORONTO. / WORTH 5¢ IN OUR LUBRITORIUM OR FOR STATION PREMIUMS. The values are in Roman numerals above CENTS in black rectangles at each corner with the lettering in the background colour of the coupon.

These coupons were also issued by the Barrie and Quebec stores.

Back:

CTM2-1: Security frame bearing the words CASH BONUS at the top and REDEEMABLE FOR MERCHANDISE AT GASOLINE BAR OR STORE. A quality seal with a single maple leaf with "cTc" within a ring inscribed TESTED PROVEN PRODUCTS. At each side is the coupon value on a security design. A serial number, in red, is above each value. The prefix for the Barrie store has a small "L" in the serial number

    Signatures: None
Serial Number: Letter prefix with six digit number
       Imprint: British American Bank Note Company Limited Ottawa Canada

PRICING TABLE

Cat.No.	Serial Prefix	Estimate Number	Store Location	F	VF	Unc
CTM2-1	L	200000	Toronto	10.00	20.00	75.00
CTM2-2	L	N/A	Barrie	18.00	35.00	75.00
CTM2-3	N/A	N/A	Quebec		Rare	

N/A = Not Available

CTM3   COURTESY CORNERS COUPONS

In 1966 Courtesy Corners was a City Service Oil Co. franchise at Newmarket which Canadian Tire had proposed to buy and call Courtesy Corners. End of stock coupons were overprinted in anticipation of the purchase and were to be used in a local advertising campaign. The deal fell through and the franchise was sold to British Petroleum. British Petroleum at the same time was evaluating the chance of being able to market gasoline under the BP sign at CTC outlets. The Courtesy Corners overprinted coupons were never issued by Canadian Tire for distribution. Some have escaped to collectors hands.

Face:

CTM3-1: Rural scene (CT1-1-1c) 5¢ coupon overprinted on the face in black. The 5¢ denomination is cancelled by a single diagonal line and the words SEE REVERSE printed diagonally from lower left to upper right across the coupon in black.

Back:

CTM3-1: As CT1-1 but the value counters 5¢ overprinted with a black figure "1" and the words LUBE CHIT near each counter. Across the center, in black, the words "Good only at COURTESY CORNERS LUBRITORIUM / Toward Greasing and Oil Change"

Face:

CTM3-3: Rural scene (CT1-5c) 25¢ coupon overprinted on the face in black. The 25¢ denomination is cancelled by a single diagonal line and the words SEE REVERSE printed diagonally from lower left to upper right across the coupon in black.

Back:

CTM3-3 As CT1-5c but the value counters 25¢ overprinted with a black figure "5" and the words LUBE CHIT near each counter. Across the center, in black, the words "Good only at COURTESY CORNERS LUBRITORIUM / Toward Greasing and Oil Change"

    Signature: F. Sasaki, Treasurer and A. Billes, President
    Imprint: British American Bank Note Company Limited

      Varieties:
         A. The overprint SEE REVERSE on CT1-1 is found printed as a mirror image.

PRICING TABLE

Cat.No.	Coupon Value	Overprint Description	F	VF	Unc
CTM3-1	1 Lube	Red overprint / black back	25.00	50.00	100.00
CTM3-2	1 Lube	Black overprint / black back	30.00	60.00	125.00
CTM3-2A	1 Lube	Black overprint / black back	25.00	50.00	100.00
CTM3-3	5 Lube	Black overprint / black back	35.00	75.00	150.00

CTM4   TORONTO OIL OR GREASING COUPON

In 1966 Coupons were mailed out with a lettter advertising oil and grease jobs by a local Toronto franchise. The reason for the issue of these overprinted coupons was regular coupons could only be redeemed for merchandise at the store. These overprinted special coupons were redeemable at the gas bar.

Face:

CTM4-1: As CT3-1-1d with centre serial number but the 5¢ value boxes are cancelled out with an "X" and SEE REVERSE printed diagonally across the face in red. The face of the 10¢ and 25¢ coupons were also overprinted in red.

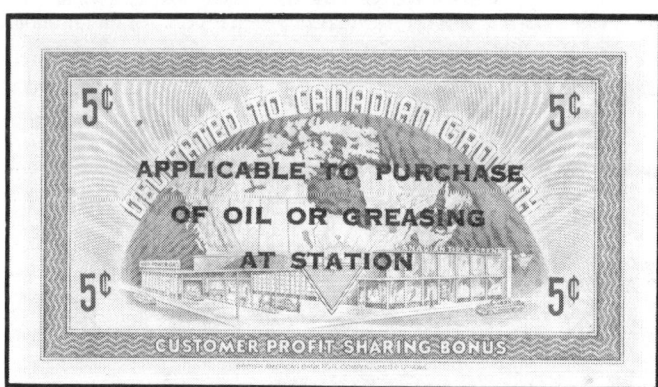

Back:

CTM4-1: Has the words "APPLICABLE TO PURCHASE / OF OIL OR GREASING / AT STATION", overprinted in red. The 10¢ and 25¢ coupons have backs overprinted in black.

    Signatures: F. Sasaki, Treasurer and A. Billes, President
    Imprint: British American Bank Note Company Limited Ottawa

PRICING TABLE

Cat.No.	Coupon Value	Overprint Colour	F	VF	Unc
CTM4-1	5¢	Red face; red back, CT3-1d	5.00	10.00	25.00
CTM4-2	10¢	Red face; black back, CT3-2d	5.00	10.00	25.00
CTM4-3	25¢	Red face; black back, CT3-5d	5.00	10.00	25.00

CTM5   ANNIVERSARY DISCOUNT GASOLINE COUPON

Issued by the Associate Store and redeemed at the gas bar and intended for use from January 1, 1972 to January 1, 1973. Use actually extended to December 31, 1973. The price of regular gasoline was 54.9¢ a gallon.

Face:

CTM5-1:   A security frame having the triangle logo at the top and the imprint CANADIAN BANK NOTE CO. below. In the upper left and upper right are "5%" CASH/DISCOUNT and 5% DE RABAIS/COMPTANT. Across the centre the words CANADIAN TIRE ANNIVERSARY COUPON, with gas pump above. Below the center the words GASOLINE/DISCOUNT, and ONLY ONE COUPON MAY BE USED/FOR ANY ONE PURCHASE OF GASOLINE, and UN SEUL COUPON - REDUCTION/PAR ACHAT D'ESSENCE. All on an underprint of triangle and maple leaves, in green.

Back:

CTM5-1:   Within a security frame, a gasoline pump with GASOLINE/DISCOUNT below and "5%" at each side. An 8 digit red serial number, with no prefix is above each "5%". Below, EXPIRES JANUARY 1, 1973 - EXPIRE LE 1er JANVIER 1973. In upper left, ADD THIS BONUS COUPON TO/YOUR REGULAR GAS BAR DISCOUNT COUPONS/AND GET EVEN BIGGER SAVINGS. French text in upper right.

Signatures: F.Y. Sasaki, Treasurer and Dean Muncaster, President
Imprint: Canadian Bank Note Co.

PRICING TABLE

Cat.No.	Percentage	Coupon Colour	Estimate Number	V	VF	Unc
CTM5-1	5	Green	3950000	5.00	10.00	20.00

STORE COUPONS
CT21 to CT28

The vignette of Sandy McTire was engraved by Gordon Yorke of the British American Bank Note Company.

All coupons in the Scotsman series are printed 133mm by 55mm, and cut to 140mm x 70mm resulting in 3.5mm X 7.5mm border. The catalogue numbers of the Scotsman series start at CT-20 to provide for possible additions in the gas bar series.

CT21   FIRST ISSUE — 1961
        SEAL DESIGN

"Tested Proven Products" Seal on Back

The Associate Stores issued more 5¢ and 10¢ discount coupons as needed. This series shows that after 10 million coupons H and L prefixes were added.

Face:

CT21-2:   Security frame bearing the words CASH BONUS, BON D'ACHAT, ECONOMIE! SECURITE!, SAVE SAFELY, CUSTOMER PROFIT SHARING BONUS. The words CANADIAN TIRE CORP'N LTD. over the lined triangle logo. Sandy McTire is to the left. On ribbons, the words REDEEMABLE IN MERCHANDISE - REMBOURSABLE EN MARCHANDISE, and, AT CANADIAN TIRE STORE OR GAS BAR, and, AU MAGASIN OU BAR D'ESSENCE CANADIAN TIRE. The coupon value is within lined boxes in each corner having a black background. Coupon background is "cTc" in circles.

Back:

CT21-2:   Security frame bearing the words CASH BONUS at the top and REDEEMABLE FOR MERCHANDISE AT GASOLINE BAR OR STORE. A quality seal with a single maple leaf with "cTc" within a ring inscribed TESTED PROVEN PRODUCTS. At each side is the coupon value on a security design. A serial number, in red, is above each value. Gordon Yorke, BABNC, engraved the plates.

28

SPECIMEN COUPON

Face:
CT21-2SP

Back:
CT21-2SP

The word SPECIMEN is printed below the company name on the front. On the back the red serial number has a value prefix and 7 zeros. On some coupons the word SPECIMEN is printed below each denomination, on others the word is omitted. Coupons are perforated through the signatures.

    Signatures: F. Saski, Treasurer and A. Billes, President
                      Error: correct spelling is 'Sasaki'

      Imprint:
         Back: British American Bank Note Company Limited Ottawa Canada
Serial Number: Prefix letter with seven digits

TECHNICAL DATA

Cat.No.	Coupon Value	Colour	Serial Number Low	Est. Low	High	Estimate of Quantity Printed
CT21-1	3¢	Blue	A0033244	A0000001	A9953515	10,000,000
CT21-1SP	3¢	Blue	A0000000			Unknown
CT21-2	5¢	Green	B0013397	B0000001	B9966496	10,000,000
CT21-2SP	5¢	Green	B0000000			Unknown
CT21-3	5¢	Grey	H0026906	H0000001	H9998490	10,000,000
CT21-4	10¢	Red	C1151759	C0000001	C9964063	10,000,000
CT21-4SP	10¢	Red	C0000000			Unknown
CT21-5	10¢	Red	L0038662	L0000001	L9977067	10,000,000
CT21-6	25¢	Violet	D0231759	D0000001	D8335669	840,000
CT21-6SP	25¢	Violet	D0000000			Unknown
CT21-7	50¢	Green	E0154896	E0000001	E4000887	4,000,000
CT21-7SP	50¢	Green	E0000000			Unknown
CT21-8	$1.00	Green	F0016452	F0000001	F1896925	2,000,000
CT21-8SP	$1.00	Green	F0000000			Unknown

PRICING TABLE

Cat. No.	Coupon Value	Serial Prefix	Coupon Colour	F	VF	Unc
CT21-1	3¢	A	Blue	3.00	5.00	15.00
CT21-1SP	3¢	A	Blue		Specimen	100.00
CT21-2	5¢	B	Green	3.00	5.00	15.00
CT21-2SP	5¢	B	Green		Specimen	100.00
CT21-3	5¢	H	Grey	3.00	5.00	15.00
CT21-4	10¢	C	Red	3.00	5.00	15.00
CT21-4SP	10¢	C	Red		Specimen	100.00
CT21-5	10¢	L	Red	3.00	5.00	15.00
CT21-6	25¢	D	Violet	4.00	7.00	20.00
CT21-6SP	25¢	D	Violet		Specimen	100.00
CT21-7	50¢	E	Green	4.00	7.00	20.00
CT21-7SP	50¢	E	Green		Specimen	100.00
CT21-8	$1.00	F	Green	6.00	10.00	30.00
CT21-8SP	$1.00	F	Green		Specimen	100.00

CT22 SECOND ISSUE — 1972
50TH ANNIVERSARY SERIES

The company appears to be confused regarding its origin. The company catalogue for 1953 proclaims their 40th Anniversary and recognizes their date of origin as 1913 when John Billes started the company (see postage meter ad on Anniversary envelope). Indeed, a ceremonial lunch was held March 25, 1953, to record the fact. The 1972 catalogue depicts the 50th Anniversary logo and recognizes the date of origin as 1922 when Alfred Billes joined the company (complete company history on page ii). This is a short series.

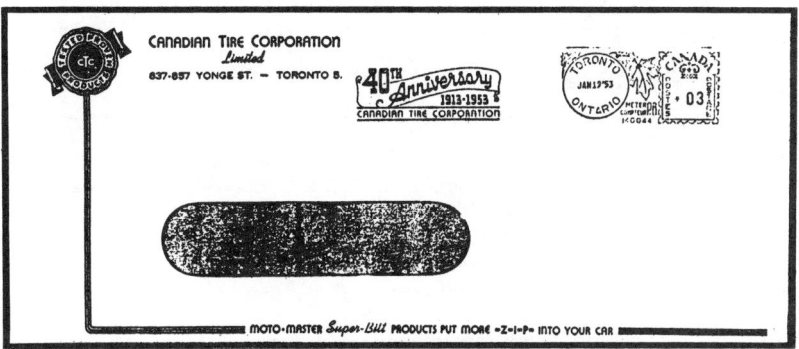

Envelope showing 40th Anniversary as 1913 to 1953.

Face:

CT22-1-2: The security frame is as CT21. Coupon values in each corner are smaller in size and the same background colour as the coupon. Background colour is imparted by a series of single coloured maple leaves. The name CANADIAN TIRE / CORPORATION LIMITED is to left of the company triangle logo. The 50th anniversary logo is at left. The "redeemable" notice is the same as CT21 but not lined.

Back:

CT22-1-2: The back features the new Toronto, Sheppard Avenue Associate store (No. 264) with Pit Stop and garage. The company triangle logo and company sign are at left and right. Wording on the security frame is as CT21. Values in each corner are not boxed. The background is single maple leaves. Two red serial numbers are at the top of the coupon.

CT22-1   Lined Counters in Tinted Counter Blocks

Signatures: F.Y. Sasaki, Treasurer and Dean Muncaster, President
Imprint: British American Bank Note Company Limited Ottawa Canada
Serial Number: Prefix letter with seven digits

TECHNICAL DATA

	Coupon			Serial Number		Estimate of
Cat.No.	Value	Colour	Low	Est. Low	High	Quantity Printed
CT22-1-1	3¢	Blue	R0017804	R0000001	R0224159	225,000
CT22-1-2	5¢	Green	S0009922	S0000001	S0463885	465,000
CT22-1-3	10¢	Red	T0029512	T0000001	T0553779	575,000
CT22-1-4	25¢	Violet	U0012054	U0000001	U0167206	175,000
CT22-1-5	50¢	Brown	V0016654	V0000001	V0055487	60,000
CT22-1-6	$1.00	Grey	W0003341	W0000001	W0019500	20,000

PRICING TABLE

Cat. No	Coupon Value	Serial Prefix	Coupon Colour	F	VF	Unc
CT22-1-1	3¢	R	Blue	10.00	20.00	50.00
CT22-1-2	5¢	S	Green	8.00	15.00	40.00
CT22-1-3	10¢	T	Red	8.00	15.00	40.00
CT22-1-4	25¢	U	Violet	12.00	20.00	60.00
CT22-1-5	50¢	V	Brown	15.00	25.00	75.00
CT22-1-6	$1.00	W	Grey	20.00	35.00	100.00

Note: An inverted "M" was used as a "W" on some of the $1.00 W prefix coupons.

CT22-2 Black Counters in Tinted Counter Blocks

Face:

CT22-2-2: White values were harder for cashiers to see so the coupon was modified. The security frame is as CT21. Coupon values in each corner are smaller in size and are solid black in colour. Background colour is imparted by a series of single coloured maple leaves. The underprint was also changed from white with coloured maple leaves to coloured with white outlined maple leaves. The name CANADIAN TIRE / CORPORATION LIMITED is to left of the company triangle logo. The 50th anniversary logo is at left. The "redeemable" notice is the same as CT21.

Back:

CT22-2-2: The back features the new Sheppard Avenue, Toronto, Associate Store ((No. 264) with Pit Stop and garage. The company triangle logo and company sign are at left and right. Wording on the security frame is as CT21. Values in each corner are not boxed. The background is single maple leaves. Two red serial numbers are at the top of the coupon.

Signatures: F. Y. Sasaki, Treasurer, and Dean Muncaster, President
Imprint: British American Bank Note Company Ottawa Canada
Serial Number: Prefix letter with seven digits. The serial numbers of CT22-1 cross over and continue into CT22-2 at about:

VALUE	PREFIX	CT22-1 to CT22-2
3¢	R	R0225000
5¢	S	S0465000
10¢	T	T0575000
25¢	U	U0175000
50¢	V	V0060000
$1.00	W	W0020000

TECHNICAL DATA

Cat.No.	Coupon Value	Colour	Serial Number Low	Est. Low	High	Estimate of Quantity Printed
CT22-2-1	3¢	Blue	R0268343	R0225000	R1734916	1,510,000
CT22-2-2	5¢	Green	S0470344	S0465000	S3384992	2,930,000
CT22-2-3	10¢	Red	T0601470	T0575000	T4036790	3,470,000
CT22-2-4	25¢	Violet	U0206446	U0175000	U1308520	1,140,000
CT22-2-5	50¢	Brown	V0067700	V0060000	V052056	465,000
CT22-2-6	$1.00	Grey	W0020965	W0020000	W0089543	70,000

PRICING TABLE

Cat. No.	Coupon Value	Serial Prefix	Coupon Colour	F	VF	Unc
CT22-2-1	3¢	R	Blue	5.00	9.00	25.00
CT22-2-2	5¢	S	Green	4.00	7.00	20.00
CT22-2-3	10¢	T	Red	3.00	5.00	15.00
CT22-2-4	25¢	U	Violet	5.00	9.00	25.00
CT22-2-5	50¢	V	Brown	8.00	15.00	40.00
CT22-2-6	$1.00	W	Grey	15.00	25.00	75.00

CT23

THIRD ISSUE —1974
TRIANGLE LOGO DESIGN

Tinted Counters on Black Framed Counter Blocks

Face:

CT23-2:   A security frame bearing the words CASH BONUS above and BON D'ACHAT below. Values are in lined rectangles at each corner. The underprint consists of triangles and maple leaves. Superimposed on a dotted triangle is the name CANADIAN TIRE/CORPORATION LIMITED. Below, on a double lined ribbon, REDEEMABLE IN MERCHANDISE - REMBOURSABLE EN MARCHANDISE. Below, on another ribbon, AT CANADIAN TIRE STORE OR GAS BAR - AU MAGASIN OU BAR D'ESSENCE CANADIAN TIRE.

Back:

CT23-2:   On a security device, a dotted triangle with values at each side. Above the values, a serial number in red, with two prefix letters. The security frame bears the statement REDEEMABLE FOR MERCHANDISE AT GASOLINE BAR OR STORE, and, REMBOURSABLE EN MARCHANDISE AU BAR D'ESSENCE OU AU MAGASIN.

SPECIMEN COUPON:

Face:
CT23-24SP

Back:
CT23-24SP

Specimen coupons have the word SPECIMEN in red thin non-serifed capital letters at an angle over the corporate triangle on the face. The back has the value prefix and seven zeros. Some coupons have a control number in the outer border. They are perforated near the bottom.

        Signatures: F.Y. Sasaki, Treasurer and Dean Muncaster, President
            Imprint: Canadian Bank Note
Serial Numbers: Two letter prefixes with seven digit numbers. The main serial
                         numbers in CT-23 are red and are fluorescent. An orange
                         serial number variety exists in some prefix letters but these
                         are not fluorescent.

Varieties:

R: Asterick or replacement coupons exist. They have an * before the prefix letters and are denoted in the pricing table as "R"

A: Orange Serial Numbers:
The standard colour of the serial numbers in this series is red. However orange serial numbers exist in prefix numbers AM, BM, CM, DM, EM and ZN.

CT23-2 Large Serial Number (Red)   CT23-2B Small Serial Number (Orange)

B. Serial Number Variety:
Coupon CT23-2B is the small serial number variety.

C. Colour Variation:
Early printings of the 3¢ note were issued in a light blue background tint.

TECHNICAL DATA

Cat.No.	Coupon Value	Colour	Serial Number Low	Est. Low	High	Estimate of Quantity Printed
CT23-1	3¢	Blue	AN0018348	AN0000001	AN9994595	8,300,000
CT23-1R	3¢	Blue	*AN	Unknown		Est. 6,700
CT23-1SP	3¢	Blue	AN0000000		Unknown	
CT23-1C	3¢	Lt. Blue	AN1736020	AN0000001	AN3358005	1,600,000
CT23-2	3¢	Blue	XN0016788	XN0000001	XN3555045	3,577,000
CT23-2B	3¢	Blue	XN3578596	XN0000001	XN3848979	275,000
CT23-3	5¢	Green	AM0084734	AM0000001	AM9136074	8,550,000
CT23-3A	5¢	Green	AM6286319	AM0000001	AM7747879	1,450,000
CT23-4	5¢	Green	BN0146309	BN0000001	BN9962364	10,000,000
CT23-4SP	5¢	Green	BN0000000			Unknown
CT23-5	5¢	Green	HN0106516	HN0000001	HN9981842	10,000,000
CT23-5R	5¢	Green	*HN	Unknown		Est. 18,000
CT23-6	5¢	Green	QN0048397	QN0000001	QN9958461	10,000,000
CT23-7	5¢	Green	TN0003118	TN0000001	TN9906594	10,000,000
CT23-8	10¢	Red	CM0173495	CM0000001	CM9860900	9,000,000
CT23-8A	10¢	Red	CM Unk.		CM9840000	1,000,000
CT23-9	10¢	Red	EM0021950	EM0000001	EM3271836	2,355,000
CT23-9A	10¢	Red	EM017000	EM0000001	EM1092006	9151000
CT23-10	10¢	Red	CN0004304	CN0000001	CN9989444	10,000,000
CT23-10SP	10¢	Red	CN0000000			Unknown
CT23-11	10¢	Red	GN0091071	GN0000001	GN9955667	10,000,000
CT23-12	10¢	Red	PN0059013	PN0000001	PN9981539	10,000,000
CT23-12R	10¢	Red	*PN	Unknown		Est. 17,400
CT23-13	10¢	Red	SN0002905	SN0000001	SN9985886	10,000,000
CT23-14	10¢	Red	UN0007857	UN0000001	UN9923146	10,000,000
CT23-15	10¢	Red	YN0008554	YN0000001	9904225	10,000,000
CT23-16	25¢	Violet	BM0049091	BM0000001	BM4793393	3,300,000
CT23-16A	25¢	Violet	BM1938338	BM0000001	BM3445375	1,500,000
CT23-17	25¢	Violet	DN0006303	DN0000001	DN9997521	10,000,000
CR23-17R	25¢	Violet	*DN	Unknown		Est. 8,400
CT23-17SP	25¢	Violet	DN00000000			Unknown
CT23-18	25¢	Violet	RN0252083	RN0000001	QN9992274	10,000,000
CT23-19	25¢	Violet	WN0003285	WN0000001	WN9975073	10,000,000
CT23-20	50¢	Brown	EN0016701	EN0000001	EN998597	10,000,000
CT23-20R	50¢	Brown	*EN	Unknown		Est. 4,500
CT23-20SP	50¢	Brown	EN0000000			Unknown
CT23-21	50¢	Brown	ZN0024578	ZN0000001	ZN6967796	6,800,000
CT23-22	50¢	Brown	RED-N0 FL			2,000,000
CT23-23	$1.00	Grey	DM0015090	DM0000001	DM1625164	1,175,000
CT23-23A	$1.00	Grey	DM0439721	DM0000001	DM889226	450,000
CT23-24	$1.00	Grey	FN0011092	FN0000001	FN9998200	10,000,000
CT23-24R	$1.00	Grey	*FN	Unknown		Est. 7,200
CT23-24SP	$1.00	Grey	FN0000000			Unknown

Note: "A" in the Cat.No. denotes an orange serial number:

PRICING TABLE

Cat. No.	Coupon Value	Serial Prefix	Coupon Colour	F	VF	Unc
CT23-1	3¢	AN	Blue	2.00	4.00	10.00
CT23-1R	3¢	AN	Blue	9.00	16.00	40.00
CT23-1SP	3¢	AN	Blue		Specimen	60.00
CT23-1D	3¢	AN	Lt blue	3.00	6.00	15.00
CT23-2	3¢	XN	Blue	3.00	6.00	15.00
CT23-2B	3¢	XN	Blue	4.00	7.00	20.00
CT23-3	5¢	AM	Green	1.75	3.00	8.00
CT23-3A	5¢	AM	Green	4.00	7.00	20.00
CT23-4	5¢	BN	Green	2.00	4.00	10.00
CT23-4SP	5¢	BN	Green		Specimen	60.00
CT23-5	5¢	HN	Green	2.00	4.00	10.00
CT23-5R	5¢	HN	Green	6.00	12.00	30.00
CT23-6	5¢	QN	Green	2.00	4.00	10.00
CT23-7	5¢	TN	Green	2.00	4.00	10.00
CT23-8	10¢	CM	Red	1.75	3.00	8.00
CT23-8A	10¢	CM	Red	4.00	7.00	20.00
CT23-9	10¢	EM	Red	3.00	6.00	15.00
CT23-9A	10¢	EM	Red	4.00	7.00	20.00
CT23-10	10¢	CN	Red	2.00	4.00	10.00
CT23-10SP	10¢	CN	Red		Specimen	60.00
CT23-11	10¢	GN	Red	2.00	4.00	10.00
CT23-12	10¢	PN	Red	2.00	4.00	10.00
CT23-12R	10¢	PN	Red	6.00	12.00	30.00
CT23-13	10¢	SN	Red	2.00	4.00	10.00
CT23-14	10¢	UN	Red	2.00	4.00	10.00
CT23-15	10¢	YN	Red	2.00	4.00	10.00
CT23-16	25¢	BM	Violet	3.00	6.00	15.00
CT23-16A	25¢	BM	Violet	4.00	7.00	20.00
CT23-17	25¢	DN	Violet	2.00	4.00	10.00
CR23-17R	25¢	DN	Violet	9.00	16.00	45.00
CT23-17SP	25¢	DN	Violet		Specimen	60.00
CT23-18	25¢	RN	Violet	2.00	4.00	10.00
CT23-19	25¢	WN	Violet	2.00	4.00	10.00
CT23-20	50¢	EN	Brown	2.00	4.00	10.00
CT23-20R	50¢	EN	Brown	12.00	20.00	60.00
CT23-20SP	50¢	EN	Brown		Specimen	60.00
CT23-21	50¢	ZN	Brown	2.00	4.00	8.00
CT23-22A	50¢	ZN	Brown	3.00	6.00	15.00
CT23-23	$1.00	DM	Grey	4.00	7.00	20.00
CT23-23A	$1.00	DM	Grey	5.00	10.00	25.00
CT23-24	$1.00	FN	Grey	2.00	4.00	10.00
CT23-24R	$1.00	FN	Grey	6.00	16.00	60.00
CT23-24SP	$1.00	FN	Grey		Specimen	60.00

CT24   FOURTH ISSUE — 1976
MONTREAL "OLYMPIADE XXI OLYMPIAD"

Tinted Counters in Solid Colour Circles

The Canadian Olympic Committee asked the corporation for a donation of $50,000 in support of the XXI Olympiade Summer Games at Montreal in 1976. In lieu of the donation the corporation donated the proceeds from the use of this series of special coupons to the Olympic Committee. The face value of coupons issued was $1,925,000. This was the last issue that was redeemable at the gas bar.

Face:

CT24-2: Scalloped security border with CASH BONUS at top and BON D'ACHAT at the bottom. Coupon values in circles at each corner. Background is a pattern of maple leaves. At left, in an oval, a large maple leaf and the five ring olympic symbol below. The company name is on top of the company triangle logo with single maple leaf. In a black background, the words REDEEMABLE IN MERCHANDISE - REMBOURSABLE EN MARCHANDISE; below, AT CANADIAN TIRE STORE OR GAS BAR - AU MAGASIN OU BAR D'ESSENCE CANADIAN TIRE.

Back:

CT24-2: Scalloped security border with REDEEMABLE FOR MERCHANDISE AT GASOLINE BAR OR STORE above, and, REMBOURSABLE EN MARCHANDISE AU BAR D'ESSENCE OU AU MAGASIN below. Central is the triangle company logo with a runner carrying an olympic flame behind. On a security design the coupon value is on each side of the triangle. Below the triangle the words OLYMPIADE XXI OLYMPIAD. Above each coupon value is a red serial number.

SPECIMEN COUPON

Face:

CT24-5SP

Back:

CT24-5SP

Specimen coupons have the word SPECIMEN across the face. On the back the value prefix is followed by seven zeros. These coupons are punch cancelled and exist for each denomination.

        Signatures: F.Y. Sasaki, Treasurer and Dean Muncaster, President
           Imprint: Canadian Bank Note
 Serial Numbers: The two letter prefix has a seven digit number. The Olympic Issue was a short series. The total issue is noted below.

TECHNICAL DATA

Cat.No.	Coupon Value	Coupon Colour	Serial Number Low	Serial Number Est. Low	Serial Number High	Estimate of Quantity Printed
CT24-1	3¢	Blue	JN0002846	JN0000001	JN0893590	900,000
CT24-1SP	3¢	Blue	JN0000000			Unknown
CT24-2	5¢	Green	KN0000068	KN0000001	KN3170990	3,180,000
CT24-2SP	5¢	Green	KN0000000			Unknown
CT24-3	10¢	Orange	LN0005251	LN0000001	LN3884220	3,885,000
CT24-3SP	10¢	Orange	LN0000000			Unknown
CT24-4	25¢	Violet	MN0002147	MN0000001	MN1847965	1,850,000
CT24-4SP	25¢	Violet	MN0000000			Unknown
CT24-5	50¢	Brown	NN0002846	NN0000001	NN0765533	800,000
CT24-5SP	50¢	Brown	NN0000000			Unknown
CT24-6	$1.00	Grey	ON0001216	ON0000001	ON0489089	500,000
CT24-6SP	$1.00	Grey	ON0000000			Unknown

PRICING TABLE

Cat. No.	Coupon Value	Serial Prefix	Coupon Colour	F	VF	Unc
CT24-1	3¢	JN	Blue	4.00	8.00	15.00
CT24-1SP	3¢	JN	Blue		Specimen	75.00
CT24-2	5¢	KN	Green	2.00	4.00	10.00
CT24-2SP	5¢	KN	Green		Specimen	75.00
CT24-3	10¢	LN	Orange	2.00	4.00	10.00
CT24-3SP	10¢	LN	Orange		Specimen	75.00
CT24-4	25¢	MN	Violet	3.00	5.00	12.00
CT24-4SP	25¢	MN	Violet		Specimen	75.00
CT24-5	50¢	NN	Brown	4.00	8.00	15.00
CT24-5SP	50¢	MN	Brown		Specimen	75.00
CT24-6	$1.00	ON	Grey	5.00	10.00	20.00
CT24-6SP	$1.00	ON	Grey		Specimen	75.00

CT25

FIFTH ISSUE — 1985
MODIFIED TRIANGLE LOGO DESIGN

White Counters in Black Framed Circles

Fred Sasaki retired from the Corporation on August 31, 1987, after 42 years of service. He had been appointed Vice President of Finance and Treasurer in 1968.

Face:

CT25-1-1: Security frame with CANADIAN TIRE CORPORATION, LIMITED above, and LA SOCIÉTE CANADIAN TIRE, LIMITEE below. Sandy McTire to left, the corporation triangle logo with REDEEMABLE IN MERCHANDISE REMBOURSABLE EN MARCHANDISE below and AT CANADIAN TIRE STORES - AUX MAGASINS CANADIAN TIRE on a folded ribbon below. The words CASH BONUS and BILLET-BONI above. The coupon values are small white numerals within a black circle at each corner.

Back:

CT25-1-1: The coupon values are smaller and wider than CT24. The security frame is scalloped, and the words read REDEEMABLE FOR MERCHANDISE AT CANADIAN TIRE STORES above, and REMBOURSABLE EN MARCHANDISE AUX MAGASINS CANADIAN TIRE below. Issued in early 1986.

    Signature: F.Y. Sasaki, Treasurer
    Imprint: Printed In Canada - © 1985 Canadian Bank Note Company. Limited.
             - Imprime Au Canada.

CT25-1   Large Red Serial Number - One Signature

CT25-1 Large Serial Number, 4mm

Serial Number: Large red seven digit serial number with two prefix letters. This serial number is 4mm high

Varieties:
A. Error Prefix: 25¢ violet coupon exists with an "AZ" error prefix.

TECHNICAL DATA

Cat.No.	Coupon Value	Coupon Colour	Serial Number Low	Serial Number Est. Low	Serial Number High	Estimate of Quantity Printed
CT25-1-1	5¢	Green	AZ0042983	AZ0000001	AZ4283953	4,290,000
CT26-1-2	10¢	Red	BY0155392	BY0000001	BY3599559	4,000,000
CT25-1-2	10¢	Red	BZ0010809	BZ0000001	BZ6421325	6,500,000
CT25-1-3	25¢	Violet	CZ0007290	CZ0000001	CZ3513130	3,700,000
CT25-1-3A	25¢	Violet	AZ			Unknown
CT25-1-4	50¢	Brown	DZ0021791	DZ0000001	DZ2573241	2,850,000
CT25-1-5	$1.00	Grey	EZ0000425	EZ0000001	EZ2555900	2,560,000

PRICING TABLE

Cat. No.	Coupon Value	Serial Prefix	Coupon Colour	F	VF	Unc
CT25-1-1	5¢	AZ	Green	1.00	2.00	5.00
CT25-1-2	10¢	BZ	Red	1.00	2.00	5.00
CT25-1-3	25¢	CZ	Violet	1.00	3.00	6.00
CT25-1-3A	25¢	AZ	Violet		Rare	
CT25-1-4	50¢	DZ	Brown	2.00	4.00	7.00
CT25-1-5	$1.00	EZ	Grey	3.00	4.00	7.00

CT25-2   Small Red Serial Number - One Signature

CT25-2-1 Small Serial Number, 3mm

Serial Number: Small red seven digit serial number wit two prefix letters. This serial number is 3mm high

TECHNICAL DATA

Cat.No.	Coupon Value	Coupon Colour	Serial Number Low	Serial Number Est. Low	Serial Number High	Estimate of Quantity Printed
CT25-2-1	5¢	Green	AZ4290854	AZ0000001	AZ9101407	4,910,000
CT25-2-2	10¢	Red	BY0155392	BY0000001	BY3599559	4,000,000
CT25-2-3	10¢	Red	BZ6579833	BZ0000001	BZ9981249	3,500,000
CT25-2-4	25¢	Violet	CZ3811914	CZ0000001	CZ8110293	4,150,000
CT25-2-5	25¢	Brown	DZ2589872	DZ0000001	DZ5344076	2,820,000
CT25-2-6	50¢	Grey	EZ2593774	EZ0000001	EZ4787698	2,440,000

PRICING TABLE

Cat. No.	Coupon Value	Serial Prefix	Coupon Colour	F	VF	Unc
CT25-2-1	5¢	AZ	Green	1.00	2.00	5.00
CT25-2-2	10¢	BY	Red	1.00	2.00	5.00
CT25-2-3	10¢	BZ	Red	1.00	2.00	5.00
CT25-2-4	25¢	CZ	Violet	1.00	2.00	5.00
CT25-2-5	50¢	DZ	Brown	1.50	3.00	6.00
CT25-2-6	$1.00	EZ	Grey	1.50	3.00	6.00

CT25-3 Small Serial Number - Two Signatures

Face:
CT25-3-1

    Signatures: Douglas Heuman, Treasurer-Trésorier and Dean Grousman, President-Président
    Imprint: Printed In Canada - ©1985 Canadian Bank Note Company, Limited. Imprime Au Canada. This issue was introduced early in 1987.
    Serial Number: Two prefix letters with seven digits in red.
    Varieties:

Normal "C"

Plugged "C"

    A. Plugged "C" of SOCIETE variety occurs on some prefixes AY, BY, CZ and DZ.

TECHNICAL DATA

Cat.No.	Coupon Value	Coupon Colour	Serial Number Low	Serial Number Est. Low	Serial Number High	Estimate of Quantity Printed
CT25-3-1	5¢	Green	AY0034465	AY0000001	AY2224792	2,300,000
CT25-3-1A	5¢	Green	AY		AY	Inc. above
CT25-3-2	5¢	Green	AZ9235446	AZ0000001	AZ9956299	800,000
CT25-3-3	10¢	Red	BX0000001		BX0004000	4,000
CT25-3-4	10¢	Red	BY4148517	BY0000001	BY9999633	6,000,000
CT25-3-4A	10¢	Red	BY		BY	Inc. above
CT25-3-5	25¢	Violet	CY0063953	CY0000001	CY0653000	700,000
CT25-3-5A	25¢	Violet	CY		CY	Inc. above
CT25-3-6	25¢	Violet	CZ8186682	CZ0000001	CZ9980271	1,850,000
CT25-3-7	50¢	Brown	DZ5406719	DZ0000001	DZ7291999	1,900,000
CT25-3-7A	50¢	Brown	DZ		DZ	Inc. above
CT25-3-8	$1.00	Grey	EZ5107534	EZ0000001	EZ6367705	1,500,000

PRICING TABLE

Cat. No.	Coupon Value	Serial Prefix	Coupon Colour	F	VF	Unc
CT25-3-1	5¢	AZ	Green	2.00	5.00	10.00
CT25-3-1A	5¢	AY	Green	1.00	2.00	6.00
CT25-3-2	5¢	AZ	Green	1.00	2.00	5.00
CT25-3-3	10¢	BX	Red	10.00	20.00	50.00
CT25-3-4	10¢	BY	Red	1.00	2.00	5.00
CT25-3-4A	10¢	BY	Red	1.00	2.00	5.00
CT25-3-5	25¢	CY	Violet	1.50	3.00	8.00
CT25-3-5A	25¢	CY	Violet	1.50	3.00	8.00
CT25-3-6	25¢	CZ	Violet	1.50	3.00	8.00
CT25-3-7	50¢	DZ	Brown	1.50	3.00	8.00
CT25-3-7A	50¢	DZ	Brown	1.50	3.00	8.00
CT25-3-8	$1.00	EZ	Grey	2.00	5.00	10.00

CT26

SIXTH ISSUE — 1987 MODIFIED TRIANGLE WITH WARNING

White Counters in Black Framed Circles

Face:

CT26-1: Security frame with CANADIAN TIRE CORPORATION, LIMITED above, and LA SOCIETE CANADIAN TIRE LIMITEE below. Sandy McTire to left, the corporation triangle logo with REDEEMABLE IN MERCHANDISE REMBOURSABLE EN MARCHANDISE below and ONLY AT CANADIAN TIRE STORES - UNIQUEMENT AUX MAGASINS CANADIAN TIRE on a folded ribbon below. The words CASH BONUS and BILLET-BONI above. The coupon values are white numerals in black circles at each corner.

Back:

CT26-1: The inscription reads REDEEMABLE IN MERCHANDISE ONLY AT CANADIAN TIRE STORES. The words PROPERTY OF CANADIAN TIRE CORPORATION, LIMITED, and PROPRIETE DE LA SOCIETE CANADIAN TIRE LIMITEE is below the serial numbers. Below the coupon value the words CASH BONUS COUPONS ARE REDEEMABLE IN MERCHANDISE / ONLY AT CANADIAN TIRE ASSOCIATE STORES AND ONLY IN ASSOCIATION WITH CONSUMER PURCHASES OF MERCHANDISE / OR SERVICE IN THE ORDINARY COURSE OF RETAIL BUSINESS. This warning is repeated in the French language. The 7-digit serial number is in red and is 3 mm high. The words ONLY and UNIQUEMENT have been added to the security frame.

Signatures: Douglas Heuman, Treasurer and Dean Groussman, President

Imprint:
  Back - Top: ©1987 Canadian Tire Corporation, Limited.
  - Bottom: Printed In Canada - Canadian Bank Note Company, Limited - Imprime Au Canada

CT26-1   Small Red Seven Digit Serial Number

Back:
CT26-1-1

Serial Number: Two letter prefix with a small seven digit number in red.

Varieties:

Back:
CT-26-1-8R

R. Asterisk or replacement coupons exist and are denoted in the pricing chart as 'R' catalogue numbers. In this series the asterick follows the first prefix letter.

TECHNICAL DATA

Cat.No.	Coupon Value	Colour	Serial Number Low	Est. Low	High	Estimate of Quantity Printed
CT26-1-1	5¢	Green	AX0018748	AX0000001	AX4246252	1,700,000
CT26-1-1R	5¢	Green	A*0000001		A*0012200	12,200
CT26-1-2	5¢	Green	AY2592441	AY0000001	AY9933699	7,700,000
CT26-1-3	10¢	Red	BW0080262	BW0000001	BW5608700	5,700,000
CT26-1-3R	10¢	Red	B*0000001		B*0016200	16,200
CT26-1-4	10¢	Red	BX0014590	BX0000001	BX9592836	9,996,000
CT26-1-5	25¢	Violet	CY0743460	CY0000001	CY7605374	700,000
CT26-1-5R	25¢	Violet	C*0000001		C*0004800	4,800
CT26-1-6	50¢	Brown	DY0009774	DY0000001	DY3566966	3,600,000
CT26-1-6R	50¢	Brown	D*0000001		D*0005100	5,100
CT26-1-7	50¢	Brown	DZ6745076	DZ0000001	DZ9909959	2,700,000
CT26-1-8	$1.00	Grey	EY0111244	EY0000001	EY2389039	2,400,000
CT26-1-8R	$1.00	Grey	E*0000001		E*0003900	3,900
CT26-1-9	$1.00	Grey	EZ5643361	EZ0000001	EZ9964202	3,500,000

PRICING TABLE

Cat. No.	Coupon Value	Serial Prefix	Coupon Colour	F	VF	Unc
CT26-1-1	5¢	AX	Green	.25	.50	2.00
CT26-1-1R	5¢	A	Green	10.00	30.00	50.00
CT26-1-2	5¢	AY	Green	.25	.35	1.00
CT26-1-3	10¢	BW	Red	.30	1.00	1.50
CT26-1-3R	10¢	B	Red	10.00	30.00	50.00
CT26-1-4	10¢	BX	Red	.25	.35	1.00
CT26-1-5	25¢	CY	Violet	.25	.35	1.00
CT26-1-5R	25¢	C	Violet	10.00	30.00	50.00
CT26-1-6	50¢	DY	Brown	.30	1.00	1.50
CT26-1-6R	50¢	D	Brown	10.00	30.00	50.00
CT26-1-7	50¢	DZ	Brown	.50	1.00	1.50
CT26-1-8	$1.00	EY	Grey	.30	1.00	1.50
CT26-1-8R	$1.00	E	Grey	10.00	30.00	50.00
CT26-1-9	$1.00	EZ	Grey	.30	1.00	1.50

CT26-2　　　　　　Small Red Eight Digit Serial Number

Back:
CT26-2-5

Serial Number: Printed in red with one prefix letter and an eight digit number.

Varieties:

Back:
CT26-2-2R

R. Asterick Notes exist and are denoted in the pricing chart as 'R' catalogue numbers.

Long serial number　　　　　　Short serial number
Length 22mm　　　　　　　　Length 21mm

A. **Long Serial Numbers:**
The serial number is slightly longer on some coupons than on others. This variety, due to insufficient data, has net been priced.

TECHNICAL DATA

Cat.No.	Coupon Value	Coupon Colour	Serial Number Low	Serial Number Est. Low	Serial Number High	Estimate of Quantity Printed
CT26-2-1	5¢	Green	A00746619		A01956747	2,000,000
CT26-2-1R	5¢	Green	*00000001		*00003500	Est. 3,500
CT26-2-2	10¢	Red	B06047751		B12750475	12,450,000
CT26-2-2R	10¢	Red	*00000001		*00022000	Est. 22,000
CT26-2-3	25¢	Violet	C09080134		C12457948	11,800,000
CT26-2-3R	25¢	Violet	*000000001		*00027500	Est. 27,500
CT26-2-4	50¢	Brown	D06443063		D08648726	9,000,000
CT226-2-4R	50¢	Brown	*00000001		*00010000	Est. 10,000
CT26-2-5	$1.00	Yellow	E07089486		E08445897	9,000,000
CT26-2-5R	$1.00	Yellow	*00000001		*00004000	Est. 4,000

PRICING TABLE

Cat.No.	Coupon Value	Serial Prefix	Coupon Colour	VF	Unc
CT26-2-1	5¢	A	Green	.50	1.00
CT26-2-1R	5¢	-	Green	10.00	40.00
CT26-2-2	10¢	B	Red	.25	.75
CT26-2-2R	10¢	-	Red	10.00	40.00
CT26-2-3	25¢	C	Violet	.50	1.00
CT26-2-3R	25¢	-	Violet	10.00	40.00
CT26-2-4	50¢	D	Brown	1.00	3.00
CT26-2-4R	50¢	-	Brown	10.00	40.00
CT26-2-5	$1.00	E	Yellow	2.00	4.00
CT26-2-5R	$1.00	-	Yellow	10.00	40.00

CT26-3   Small Red Ten Digit Serial Number

Back:
CT26-3-1

Serial Number: Ten digit numbers in red with no prefix letters.

TECHNICAL DATA

Cat.No.	Coupon Value	Coupon Colour	Serial Number Low	Serial Number Est. Low	Serial Number High	Estimate of Quantity Printed
CT26-3-1	10¢	Red				Est. 800,000
CT26-3-2	25¢	Violet				Est. 500,000

PRICING TABLE

Cat.No.	Coupon Value	Coupon Colour	VF	Unc
CT26-3-1	10¢	Red	1.00	3.00
CT26-3-2	25¢	Violet	1.00	4.00

CT27

SEVENTH ISSUE — 1989
MODIFIED TRIANGLE WITH WARNING

Black Counters in Grey Framed Circles

Face:

CT27-1:   Similar to CT26 but the background is darker and the signatures are different in detail and there are two more security devices - a VOID on each side of the corporation triangle background and fine lines of print with the corporation name instead of solid lines below the upper security frame, repeated eight times. Three of them do not have the word LIMITED. The value counters are black numerals on a grey background.

Back:

CT27-1:   The words ONLY and UNIQUEMENT have been added to the security frame wording. The words "Property of Canadian Tire Corporation, Limited, and Propriete de La Societe Canadian Tire Limitee" is below the serial numbers. Below the coupon value the words "Cash bonus coupons are redeemable in / merchandise / only at Canadian Tire associate stores and only in / association with consumer purchases of merchandise / or service in the ordinary course of retail business" This warning is repeated in the French language. The serial numbers are 4 mm high.

Signatures: Douglas Heuman, Treasurer, and Dean Groussman, President

Imprint :
Back   - Top: ©1989 Canadian Tire Corporation, Limited
         - Bottom: Printed In Canada - BA Banknote
                         - Imprimé Au Canada.

CT27-1 Large Red Seven Digit Serial Number

Back:
CT27-1-2

Serial Number: Seven digit red serial number with one prefix letter.

TECHNICAL DATA

Cat.No.	Coupon Value	Coupon Colour	Serial Number Low	Serial Number Est. Low	Serial Number High	Estimate of Quantity Printed
CT27-1-1	5¢	Green	A0002228	A0000001	A0597069	600,000
CT27-1-2	25¢	Violet	J 0013655	J 0000001	J 0975684	1,000,000
CT27-1-3	$1.00	Blue	Q0001572	Q0000001	Q0399833	400,000

PRICING TABLE

Cat. No.	Coupon Value	Serial Prefix	Coupon Colour	F	VF	Unc
CT27-1-1	5¢	A	Green	2.00	3.00	8.00
CT27-1-2	25¢	J	Violet	1.00	2.00	5.00
CT27-1-3	$1.00	Q	Bue	2.00	5.00	10.00

CT27-2   Large Black Seven Digit Serial Number

Back:
CT27-2-7

Serial Number: Seven digit serial number in black with one prefix letter.

TECHNICAL DATA

Cat.No.	Coupon Value	Colour	Serial Number Low	Est. Low	High	Estimate of Quantity Printed
CT27-2-1	5¢	Green	A0635223	A0600000	A9020040	9,940,000
CT27-2-2	5¢	Green	B0048027	B0000001	B0223546	400,000
CT27-2-3	10¢	Red	E0050688	E0000001	E9910015	10,000,000
CT27-2-4	10¢	Red	F0010213	F0000001	F3899779	4,000,000
CT27-2-5	25¢	Violet	J1011820	J1000000	J8400678	7,400,000
CT27-2-6	50¢	Brown	M0044241	M0000001	M4895923	5,000,000
CT27-2-7	$1.00	Blue	Q0423444	Q0400000	Q6283543	5,900,000
CT27-2-8	$2.00	Orange	T00000626	T0000001	T0025000	Est. 500,000

PRICING TABLE

Cat. No.	Coupon Value	Serial Prefix	Coupon Colour	F	VF	Unc
CT27-2-1	5¢	A	Green	.25	.50	1.00
CT27-2-2	5¢	B	Green	1.50	3.00	6.00
CT27-2-3	10¢	E	Red	.25	.50	1.00
CT27-2-4	10¢	F	Red	.75	1.00	2.00
CT27-2-5	25¢	J	Violet	.50	.75	1.50
CT27-2-6	50¢	M	Brown	.75	1.00	2.00
CT27-2-7	$1.00	Q	Blue	1.25	1.75	3.00
CT27-2-8	$2.00	T	Orange	4.00	8.00	15.00

CT28

EIGHTH ISSUE — 1992
LARGE SANDY McTIRE DESIGN

Coloured Counters on Tinted Coloured Blocks
Small Black Serial Number

Face:
CT28-2: Sandy McTire at right, facing front. The design is in three horizontal segments. The words CANADIAN TIRE are in the upper segment. The centre segment has the company identification triangle and at left the words LA SOCIETE CANADIAN TIRE LIMITEE / CASH BONUS-BILLET-BONI / CANADIAN TIRE CORPORATION, LIMITED. In the lower segment the signatures of Stanley Pasternak Treasurer / Trésorier, and, Hugh Macaulay Chairman of the Board / Président du conseil. Below the signatures the words REMBOURSABLE EN MARCHANDISE UNIQUEMENT AUX MAGASINS CANADIAN TIRE / REDEEMABLE IN MERCHANDISE ONLY AT CANADIAN TIRE STORES. The underprint is a series of triangles, single maple leaves and a large triangle. Counters are in tall thin serified numerals in each corner.

Back:
CT28-2: The words REDEEMABLE IN MERCHANDISE ONLY AT CANADIAN TIRE STORES in the upper security frame and REMBOURSABLE EN MARCHANDISE UNIQUEMENT AUX MAGASINS CANADIAN TIRE in the lower. At centre the company logo, the triangle, maple leaf and company name. At each side, on a 3-d diamond the coupon value. Above, at centre, the words "Property of Canadian Tire Corporation, Limited/Propriété de la Société Canadian Tire Limitée" and a ten digit serial number in black at each side. Below, at left, the modified statement "Cash bonus coupons are redeemable in merchandise / only at Canadian Tire associate stores and only in / association with consumer purchases of merchandise / or service in the ordinary course of retail business". The equivalent words in French are at the right. Microprinting is the same design as on face of the coupon.

Serial Numbers: Ten digit black numbers

Imprint :
Back - Top: ©1992 Canadian Tire Corporation, Limited
       - Bottom: Printed In Canada -   ©1992 Canadian Bank Note Company, Limited
                    Imprimé Au Canada.

CT28-1   Pasternak / Macaulay Signatures

Face:
CT28-1-2R

Back:
CT28-1-2R

Signatures: Stanley Pasternak, Treasurer and Hugh Macaulay,
              Chairman of the Board

Varieties: Asterick or replacement notes exist and have the serial number
              beginning with the digit "9". These notes are denoted by an "R" in
              the pricing table.

58

PRICING TABLE

Cat.No.	Coupon Value	Coupon Colour	F	VF	UNC
CT28-1-1	5¢	Green	-	-	.50
CT28-1-1R	5¢	Green	2.50	5.00	10.00
CT28-1-2	10¢	Red	-	-	.50
CT28-1-2R	10¢	Red	2.50	5.00	10.00
CT28-1-3	25¢	Purple	-	-	1.00
CT28-1-3R	25¢	Purple	5.00	10.00	20.00
CT28-1-4	50¢	Brown	-	-	2.00
CT28-1-4R	50¢	Brown	4.00	8.00	15.00
CT28-1-5	$1.00	Blue	-	-	3.00
CT28-1-5R	$1.00	Blue	8.00	15.00	25.00

CT28-2   Kishner / Macaulay Signatures

Face:
CT28-2-1

Signatures: G.S. Kishner, Chief Financial Officer and H. Macaulay, Chairman of the Board
Varieties: Asterick or replacement notes exist and are denoted in the pricing chart as "R" catalogue numbers.

PRICING TABLE

Cat.No.	Coupon Value	Coupon Colour	F	VF	UNC
CT28-2-1	2.00	Rose	-	2.50	5.00
CT28-2-1R	2.00	Rose	12.50	25.00	50.00

Pasternak / Bachand Signatures

Face:
CT28-3-2

Signatures: Stanley Pasternak, Treasurer and Stephen E. Bachand, President and Chief Executive Officer
Varieties: Asterick or replacement notes exist and have the serial number beginning with an * asterisk followed by nine digits.

PRICING TABLE

Cat.No.	Coupon Value	Coupon Colour	F	VF	UNC
CT28-3-1	5¢	Green	-	-	.50
CT28-3-1R	5¢	Green	4.00	7.50	15.00
CT28-3-2	10¢	Red	-	-	.50
CT28-3-2R	10¢	Red	4.00	7.50	15.00
CT28-3-3	25¢	Purple	-	-	1.00
CT28-3-3R	25¢	Purple	4.00	7.50	15.00
CT28-3-4	50¢	Brown	.75	1.50	3.00
CT28-3-4R	50¢	Brown	5.00	10.00	20.00
CT28-3-5	1.00	Blue	-	1.50	3.00
CT28-3-5R	1.00	Blue	5.00	10.00	20.00
CT28-3-6	2.00	Rose	-	2.50	5.00
CT28-3-6R	2.00	Rose	5.00	10.00	20.00

Printed in Canada